## THREE HISSES FOR VILLAINY!!!

This is the sixth in the extremely successful series of melodramas by Brian J. Burton which have been performed thousands of times throughout the world.

Described as "An evening of Victorian entertainment", it consists of three original, unrelated short melodramas which, performed together with genuine Victorian ballads, constitute a programme such as might have been presented in the last century.

Although conceived as a complete show, any of the plays could be performed separately as part of an 'old-time music hall' or an evening of one-act plays.

All three settings are simplicity itself, consisting of no more than a few 'cut-outs' and tables and chairs making it ideal for presentation in theatres with lim... acilities.

... e plays can be performed by three men, three ... nd a pianist.

... ONTH TO PAY" is the traditional story of a ... ay' and a wicked landlord. (3m 3w).

... NKARD'S WIFE" is a temperance melodrama ... e so popular in the 1800s. (2m 2w).

... SY CURSE" tells the story of William Corder ... met Maria Marten. (3m 3w).

... full acting edition containing all the moves ... lete plots together with production notes by ... including advice on the style of acting and

*By the same author:*

THE HOUSE OF ROSMER
(*adapted from Ibsen*)

SWEENEY TODD THE BARBER
(*adapted from G. D. Pitt*)

THE MURDER OF MARIA MARTEN
*or*
THE RED BARN
(*based on various Victorian texts*)

EAST LYNNE *or* LADY ISABEL'S SHAME
(*based on the novel by Mrs. Henry Wood*)

LADY AUDLEY'S SECRET
*or*
DEATH IN LIME TREE WALK
*based on the novel by Mary Braddon*)

THE DRUNKARD
*or*
DOWN WITH DEMON DRINK
(*based on the version by W. H. Smith and 'a gentleman'*)

THE WOODPILE
(a modern drama in 3 acts)

Cover Photograph by Frederick Covins

ISBN – Hardback 0 85197 049 4
Paperback 0 85197 050 8

# THREE HISSES FOR VILLAINY!!!

## AN EVENING OF VICTORIAN ENTERTAINMENT

Consisting of three one-act melodramas

ONE MONTH TO PAY *or* THE SAILOR'S RETURN

THE DRUNKARD'S WIFE *or* THE TABLES TURNED

THE GYPSY CURSE *or* THE FLOWER OF THE TRIBE

by

BRIAN J. BURTON

COMBRIDGE JACKSON LIMITED

BAYLISS HOUSE
HURST STREET
BIRMINGHAM B5 4BT

*First published* 1979 *by*
COMBRIDGE JACKSON LIMITED

## INTRODUCTION

The other melodramas which have been published in this series have all been full-length and based on well-known melodramas or novels written in the 19th century. The three short plays which make up this new work are original and published for the first time in any form.

Although there were thousands of full-length melodramas written and performed in the last century, the one-act form was equally popular, often being presented as a "curtain-raiser" or an "end-piece" to the main offering of the evening. Many of the full-length melodramas were published and can still be found in libraries in the old printed versions published by Samuel French and Lacy and in the 'Dick's Penny Plays' series, but very few one-acts were printed or survive to this day.

*Three Hisses for Villainy* has been written and devised to fill that gap by providing three plays which can be performed, together with genuine Victorian ballads, to make up a full evening's entertainment. Alternatively the plays could be performed individually as part of an old-time music hall or a programme of one-act plays.

It is important to appreciate that, although they were written with the tongue fairly firmly in the cheek, it would be most unwise to treat them as burlesques. There are a number of 'cod' sketches of this kind in print. Certainly, the plays in this volume include deliberate "double entendres" which are intended to amuse a present day audience but, in the main, the intention is to recreate a similar style of play to that beloved by Victorian audiences when audience participation was an essential part of theatregoing and presentation. As such, these plays should be over-acted, in the grand manner, rather than burlesqued unmercifully.

The three most popular melodrama themes are all represented in this collection. In *One Month to Pay* or *The Sailor's Return* there is the traditional battle between a wicked landlord and the wife of his impecunious tenant with 'Jolly Jack Tar', village simpleton and 'saintly child' themes thrown in for good measure. Here, as in all three, virtue, of course, triumphs in the end.

*The Drunkard's Wife* or *The Tables Turned* is a temperance drama. These were extremely popular both in England and on the other side of the Atlantic with *The Drunkard, Ten Nights in a Bar-Room* and *Fifteen Years in a Drunkard's Life* the best known. This play employs the Victorian device of the occasional overuse of long or obscure words, which it is doubtful if the actors understood, let alone the audience. Nevertheless they were greatly enjoyed by everyone, as are the chairman's elaborate introductions in old-time music hall today.

*The Gypsy Curse* or *The Flower of the Tribe* is of another very traditional genre – the gypsy romantic drama. The interesting feature of this play is that it tells the story, recounted by one of the gypsies in *Maria Marten*, of the events that were supposed to have occurred to William Corder before he met Maria and 'foully murdered' her in the Red Barn. Although the main plot bears no relation at all to any other known play, certain minor details were suggested by *The Flowers of the Forest* a gypsy drama by John Baldwin Buckstone. This was first presented at the Adelphi Theatre in 1847 and a few lines of the dialogue and the odd phrase or two have been included, in a modified form, to enhance the apparent authenticity of the style. The words of the gypsy song are adapted from an old 19th century ballad. Appropriately, the omnibus title for this work is taken from one of the songs written for *The Murder of Maria Marten.*

BRIAN J. BURTON.

## PROGRAMME

Ballads:- Home! Sweet! Home!
J. H. Payne and Sir H. Bishop

Rocked in the cradle of the deep
E. H. Willard and J. P. Knight

The Dream — A. Bunn and M. W. Balfe

PLAY:- ONE MONTH TO PAY *or*
THE SAILOR'S RETURN — Brian J. Burton

INTERVAL

Ballads:- Father's a drunkard and Mother is dead
'Stella' and E. A. Parkhurst

Come home, Father — H. C. Work

PLAY:- THE DRUNKARD'S WIFE *or*
THE TABLES TURNED — Brian J. Burton

INTERVAL

Ballad:- The gypsy's warning — H. A. Goard

PLAY:- THE GYPSY CURSE *or*
THE FLOWER OF THE TRIBE
Brian J. Burton

THE QUEEN

THE TOTAL RUNNING TIME, EXCLUDING INTERVALS, IS ABOUT TWO HOURS

The music and lyrics of the ballads suggested are to be found in *The Parlour Song Book* (edited by Michael R. Turner) published by Michael Joseph and Pan Books.

For

GABRIELLE

# ONE MONTH TO PAY

*or*

# THE SAILOR'S RETURN

A Melodrama In One Act

*Characters*

ALICE COLLINS (A countrywoman in her late twenties)

MARY (her little daughter – can be played by an adult dressed as a child)

MRS. BENTLEY (A kind neighbour in the vale of years)

JOE (Alice's simple-minded brother)

SQUIRE MEADOWS (A black-hearted villain)

TOM (Alice's husband – a sailor)

## ONE MONTH TO PAY *or* THE SAILOR'S RETURN

Period: Late 19th century – or what you will.
The setting consists of a cut-out of a fireplace. A chair stands on each side. The exits left and right can be behind wing flats or curtains. There is a cut-out of a window left of the fireplace (or this can be imagined behind an upstage flat or curtain).

*When the curtain rises, Alice is seated left of the fireless grate with Mary at her feet on her left. Mrs. Bentley is seated on the other side of the fireplace.*

**Alice**: (*after a pause*) Ah me! Ah me! (*after another pause*) Ah me! Ah me! Ah me!

**Mrs. B**: Is there aught that troubles you, Alice my dear?

**Alice**: Alas yes, Mrs. Bentley, there is indeed. My heart is nigh to breaking, I am sore afraid, overwhelmed with apprehension and overcome with anxiety.

**Mrs. B**: As I thought, as I thought. What is the cause of your distress? Why do you not acquaint me with the reason for your woe? I am your friend, am I not?

**Alice**: Dear, kind Mrs. Bentley, you are indeed a true and loyal friend. You are my companion through the trials and tribulations of this world. Heaven knows if I could endure my weary existence were it not for your inestimable kindness. You are my mainstay, my prop, my salvation. You are my guide, my strength, my mentor. You are –

**Mrs. B**: Tut! Tut! Say no more. I would not wish you to exaggerate.

**Mary**: We must all help each other in this world. That's what they say.

**Mrs. B**: Quite right, my child, quite right. Now, Alice, tell me more of your troubles. I am most anxious to assist you if it be within my power.

**Alice**: When night has fallen and I am retired to my solitary bed, I get no respite from the cares of the day for, try as I may, sleep will not come to me. I put my weary head on the pillow but, alas, blessed oblivion will not o'ertake me. Morpheus will not wrap me in his comforting arms. I lie awake, in my lonely bed, tossing and turning, turning and tossing the whole night through, until the pale light of dawn seeps through my window shutters. Then do I drag myself from the bed of sorrow to face another awesome day, tired and exhausted.

**Mrs. B**: Tell me the cause of so much distress, dear friend. I must know if I am to aid you.
**Alice**: (*rising and moving to left of* MRS. BENTLEY) Whatever is to become of us, Mrs. Bentley? Whatever is to become of us? It is five long years since my dear husband, Tom, passed through the doorway of this sweet little cottage, kissed me and my little Mary and set off for Portsmouth to become a sailor in Her Majesty's Navy. Five years since he left England's shores bound for I know not where (*crossing* MRS. BENTLEY *to down right centre*). In all those endless years, not one single line have I received from him, not one word to inform me of his whereabouts. (*checking and turning to* MRS. BENTLEY) Whatever can he have been doing all this time? (*starts to cry*).
**Mrs. B**: (*rising and moving to* ALICE'S *left*) Poor Alice, poor dear Alice. Do not fret yourself so, my dear. He will return one day, you may be sure of that. He is but delayed. There is sure to be some simple explanation for his prolonged absence, if we but knew what it was.
**Alice**: You are wise and sagacious and know far more of the world than I, Mrs. Bentley. I have no doubt that you speak the truth and that, one day, my dear sailor husband will return to my arms and to the bosom of his family.
**Mrs. B**: Of course he will, of course. It is but a matter of time. You must have patience, my dear.
**Mary**: They do say that patience is a virtue.
**Mrs. B**: They do indeed, child.
**Alice**: But suppose . . . suppose . . .
**Mrs. B**: What is it, Alice?
**Alice**: Suppose he is too late. What then? What then?
**Mrs. B**: Too late? What mean you?
**Alice**: Suppose that before his return, I have expired from a surfeit of anguish and woe (*starts to cry again*).
**Mary**: (*rising and crossing quickly across to right of* ALICE) Do not cry, Mother dear, do not cry. My heart breaks when I see you cry. Remember, it is a long lane that has no turning. Oh, Mother!
**Alice**: (*sobbing*) What is it, Mary my child?
**Mary**: There are two tears trickling slowly down your beautiful cheeks. Wipe them away, Mother dear. Here is my hanky. It is quite clean.
**Alice**: (*taking handkerchief and wiping her eyes*) Bless you, Mary, my child, bless you. You are a great comfort to me — a great comfort.
**Mary**: You need have no cause for fear. My daddy will come back to us 'ere long. I know he will. Every night,

when I go upstairs to my little room, there is something I do.

**Alice**: What is that, child?

**Mary**: After I have washed myself and put on my night-gown, I kneel down by the side of my bed, place my hands together and say my prayers just as my father and mother taught me to do when I was little.

**Alice**: You are indeed a good girl – a good girl (*to* MRS. BENTLEY) We have been blessed with an angel child, Mrs. Bentley – an angel child.

**Mary**: I pray to Heaven to send my daddy back to us across the wide seas, safe and sound. So, you see, he is certain to return 'ere long. Of that you may be sure.

**Alice**: But what of the rent – the rent that is owing on our little nest? How can that be paid? When your dear father went away to sea, he left me all the money he had in the world. It was to provide for us whilst he was sailing the tempestuous oceans. He is a good man – a fine man.

**Mrs. B**: What happened to the money which your husband left with you? Is none of it left?

**Alice**: Alas, not a penny remains. The sum he left us would have lasted us for many a year. It was a legacy he had received from a rich uncle. But my beloved husband had left but a month before Squire Meadows visited us in this cottage, late one snowy winter's night.

**Mrs. B**: Indeed! What was the purpose of his nocturnal call?

**Alice**: To inform me that he was to increase the rent.

**Mrs. B**: To increase the rent?

**Alice**: Yes, to increase it threefold.

**Mrs. B**: Threefold?

**Alice**: Threefold. After much due consideration, I decided to acquaint him with my position.

**Mrs. B**: Yes? What did he think of that?

**Alice**: It did naught to sway him from his despicable intentions. 'Thrice the rent' he said 'Thrice, from this day forward!'

**Mrs. B**: (*moving to centre stage*) Squire Meadows said that? Tis dreadful – dreadful! I would not have believed such a thing had I not heard it from your own lips. Indeed I would not. He is a wicked man to exploit poor people in such a way.

**Mary**: But he will fail to profit from it, for ill-gotten gains never prosper, they say.

**Mrs. B**: Let us hope he does not, child. (*turning to Alice*) What did you do then?

**Alice**: Alas, what could I do? I was left with no alternative but to pay the villain the exhorbitant sum he demanded forthwith. I continued to do so for as long as the money lasted. But now it is exhausted and Squire Meadows has threatened to evict us from our home – from this dear little cottage – on the last day of this very month if the arrears have not been paid in full by then.

**Mrs. B**: From this dear little cottage where you have lived in happiness and contentment for all these years?

**Alice**: Alas, yes!

**Mrs. B**: On the last day of this very month?

**Alice**: Alas, alas, yes! He swore that unless the money was paid, and paid in full, no power on earth could force him to alter his decision and we must depart.

**Mrs. B**: Twould seem then that there would be nothing gained by asking him to take pity on you for a little longer.

**Alice**: (*crossing to right of* MRS. BENTLEY) Pity! Squire Meadows knows not the meaning of the word pity. He is a hard man. He could not be swayed by sentiment. Sometimes I think that his heart was chiselled out of a block of ice brought from the remotest regions of the arctic wastes.

**Mrs. B**: After that which you have told me, it would appear to be only too true – only too true.

**Alice**: He is the blackest villain who ever walked this earth – that he is. He is without scruples or conscience and disregards all the laws of right and justice.

**Mrs. B**: So it would seem. But, who knows, you could be mistaken. Perchance, he might have a better side to his nature. Could you not, perhaps, make a final appeal to him?

**Alice**: Better nature! He has no better nature! As I told you, 'tis of no avail. I have lost count of the number of times I have asked – nay pleaded with him but 'tis all in vain (*starts to cry again*).

**Mary**: (*moving to right of* ALICE) Wipe your eyes, Mother dear. Do they not say that even the darkest cloud has a silver lining?

**Mrs. B**: True! True!

**Mary**: Do they not say that 'tis always darkest just before the dawn?

**Mrs. B**: Indeed, yes.

**Mary**: And that hope is the poor man's bread?

**Mrs. B**: Very true, Mary my dear (*aside*) Verily, out of the mouths of babes and sucklings . . .

**Alice**: But what of my poor young brother, Joe, who lives with us here in the cottage, now that our dear father and mother have departed this life? How will he fare? Is he not simple-minded and does he not earn but a few pennies a day from his lowly labours?

**Mrs. B**: Every penny counts, Alice.

**Mary**: Do they not say that if you look after the pence, the pounds will look after themselves?

**Alice**: That is a fact I cannot deny. But, what chance have I to save those pennies? Does he not spend what he has earned by the sweat of his brow . . .

**Mrs. B**: Down at the Old Bull and Cow? So I have heard tell.

**Alice**: There is many a night when I am feared to open that door when he returns from the ale house. There is many a night when I hear his drunken singing, as he staggers up the lane, and am tempted to bar the door to him. But I cannot. Tis not his fault. The older men spend their money to buy him liquor just to hear his wild ramblings and his nonsensical songs. Too often, indeed, is he unable to climb the stairs unaided and I am obliged to put him into his bed and attend to his every need. And not a penny does he bring into this house – not a penny.

**Mrs. B**: Hush, hush! You should not talk of these matters afore the little one, bless her!

**Alice**: I am desperate. I know not which way to turn. I no longer have the means to keep body and soul together. How then, can I possibly support a child and a half-demented alcoholic brother? Poor Joe, what will become of him when we no longer have a roof over our heads? They will take him from us and put him in the workhouse. I could not bear to be parted from him. I could not bear that.

*Singing is heard offstage.* ALICE *moves to door right.* MRS. BENTLEY *sits left of fireplace.* MARY *moves to her left.*

**Alice**: Why, here is Joe now, back from the fields and waiting to be fed, you may be sure, before he sets off for his nightly session at the Old Bull and Cow. (*moves back to centre*) And not a scrap, not a morsel of food in the house.

*Enter* JOE *right. He is dressed as a country yokel in a smock, trousers tied with string below the knees and a soft hat. He is sucking a straw. He moves to right of* ALICE.

**Joe**: It be I – Joe. How be 'ee, Sister Alice? How be 'ee little Mary? How be 'ee Mrs. Bentley? How be 'ee, Joe? (*stops and scratches his head*) Eh? Now I reckons as how there be summat wrong there. What be it? (*scratches his

*head again*) Aaaah! I'se got it! I be Joe. It be I that I be talking to. And I knows how I be, I reckons. (*rubs his stomach*) I be fair famished, that I be. I'se been a-toiling away all the live-long day up in Sunnybrook meadow getting in the hay. Not one bite of food has passed these lips – not even a tough turnip or a soft swede. I'se worked up an appetite and a half, that I has. I reckons as how I could eat a big fat pig all by mysen – and that's a fact. I do hope as how 'ee's got summat good for supper tonight.
**Alice**: (*aside*) As Heaven is my witness, I know not what to say to him. I cannot tell him that I gave the last crust of bread to little Mary when she was crying with hunger. I will try to keep him occupied a little longer before I break the dreadful news to him. (*aloud*) Now, Joe, you must be very dirty after your day in the fields, so go out the back, there's a good boy, and give yourself a thorough wash from head to toe. And just you see that you wash behind your ears this time. You are forever forgetting to do so.
**Joe**: Don't 'ee talk to I as if I be a simpleton. I ain't daft 'ee knows, and that's a fact. (*going to door right and turning*) When I was a little un, our mother said as how I ought to have been called Simon. I never could fathom that one out. (*exits scratching his head*).
**Mrs. B**: (*rising and moving to left of* ALICE) Well, now must I wend my way homeward. I tell you what, Alice, I reckon if little Mary comes along home with me, I'll see if I can find a few vittals for you all, to tide off the pangs of hunger for a few more hours. I'll pack them in a basket and Mary can help me carry them back here.
**Alice**: I know not what to say.
**Mrs. B**: Then say nothing, my dear.
**Mary**: (*moving to left of* MRS. BENTLEY) They do say that silence is golden, do they not?
**Mrs. B**: Indeed they do, my dear – indeed they do.
**Alice**: May Heaven bless you, Mrs. Bentley. You are indeed the kindest of women. Were I to spend the rest of my days searching the length and breadth of the wide world I would fail to find a more saintly person than you.
**Mrs. B**: Tut, tut! Think no more of it, Alice. I am certain that I do naught but that which you would do if it were I who had the misfortune to find myself in such impecunious circumstances.
**Mary**: They do say that a friend in need is a friend indeed.
**Mrs. B**: Very true, very true.
**Alice**: Bless you once more. I will repay you a thousand fold, when my beloved husband, Tom, returns from over

the seas, where he has been for many a long day. Of that you may be sure.

**Mrs. B**: Nonsense, nonsense. I want no payment.

**Mary**: They say that virtue is its own reward, don't they, Mrs. Bentley?

**Mrs. B**: So I've heard tell. (*crossing to door right*) Come along with me then, Mary, and I will see what I can find for your supper this night. (*aside*) They shall not starve so long as I have aught to share with them – that they shall not!

**Mary**: (*crossing to* MRS. BENTLEY) Dear, kind Mrs. Bentley. When I kneel down tonight, I will say a special prayer for you.

**Mrs. B**: (*taking* MARY'S *hand*) Bless you. Come along then, dear. Say farewell to your mother.

**Mary**: Farewell, dear Mother – farewell! I will return 'ere long, never fear. Do not be concerned. Remember that absence makes the heart grow fonder. Farewell.

*Exit* MRS. BENTLEY *and* MARY.

**Alice**: (*moving to down centre – aside*) How much longer can I endure all this? Will it never end? Tis too much. The good Mrs. Bentley has been so kind to us but I cannot continue to take her food. She is but a poor widow woman and cannot afford to share her meagre lot with three extra mouths. What is to be the solution to my pressing problem? How can I escape from this sorry plight? If only Squire Meadows would show some mercy towards us in our terrible predicament.

*There is a knock at the door left.*

Ah, what is that?

*Another knock.*

Why, 'tis a knock at the door!

*Another knock.*

Another knock – but louder. Who can it be? Tis strange. It cannot be little Mary. She cannot have returned so soon. I will go to the window to ascertain the identity of this unexpected caller. (*goes to window*) Ah! Alas, 'tis he! Tis the wicked Squire Meadows. Whatever can he want with me? I will enquire. (*aloud*) What is it you want, Squire Meadows. It is not yet time. It is not the end of the month. (*aside*) But a few short days to rest secure in our little next before we are cast forth into the pitiless world.

**Squire**: (*off*) Let me in, woman! Let me in this instant. There is something I have to do.

**Alice**: (*aside*) Whatever can he mean? (*aloud*) What is it, sir? I am alone in the house. What would you have of me?

**Squire**: (*off*) I wish to have words with you.
**Alice**: (*aside*) I will let him in. There is no other option open to me. (*moves to door left*) Come then, enter! Never let it be said that I, Alice Collins, turned a living soul from my door.

SQUIRE MEADOWS *enters. He is dressed in traditional villain's costume and carries a riding crop.* ALICE *returns to centre stage.*

**Squire**: (*as he enters*) Your door, woman, did you say? Your door? Did I hear aright? Did you say that was your door? Let me tell you that you would be well advised to remember that this is my cottage and that is my door. These are my windows! This is my ceiling! This is my floor! You cannot refuse me entry to that which is mine. (*to left of* ALICE—*shouting*) Remember that—and remember it well, you miserable woman, if you know what is good for you. Do you understand? Do—you—understand!?!?!?
**Alice**: (*aside*) He appears a little put out. (*aloud*) Squire Meadows, why do you come here at this hour? What is it you wish to say to me? (*aside*) Is it possible that he has had a change of heart and has come here to acquaint me with the news that we may stay beneath this roof after all? Heaven grant that it be so! (*aloud*) Pray tell me the purpose of your visit? Tell me the nature of your intended discourse. I am weak with apprehension.
**Squire**: You wish to know the purpose of my visit, eh? Never fear, I can tell you that in no uncertain terms, with the minimum of words and with the greatest of pleasure.
**Alice**: Yes, yes? Tell me!
**Squire**: Very well. You are in debt, are you not, eh, eh, eh?
**Alice**: Yes, sir. I fear that is only too true. I cannot deny it.
**Squire**: I should think not. To deny it would be the greatest folly. As to the amount of the debt, woman – it is five pounds, eighteen shillings and sixpence three farthings. Is that not so?
**Alice**: If you say so, Squire.
**Squire**: But is that not so, woman? Answer me!
**Alice**: I believe it to be so, yes. (*aside*) Tis the sum. The amount is engraven on my heart for ever.
**Squire**: Exactly, exactly! Now – tell me – can you pay that sum? Can you settle that debt before the end of the month?
**Alice**: (*to stage right*) I cannot! I cannot! Indeed, you know I cannot. Did I not say so when you called before? Why have you come to torment me once more? Where should I find such a sum? Did I not tell you that all the money left

with me by my dear husband, Tom, when he left to serve Her Majesty, you have had of me – every penny? I have not so much as a farthing to bless myself with. I can do naught else but throw myself on your mercy.
**Squire**: Exactly, exactly. That is what I thought you might say. That is why I have come to see you again on the matter. I have been thinking it over very carefully and have a little proposition to put to you.
**Alice**: A proposition? (*aside*) I wonder what it could be.
**Squire**: Yes. I am a most generous man. I have a heart of gold. I am full of the milk of human kindness. Now, I'll tell you what I will do for you. (*approaching* ALICE) You are a provocative wench, are you not? You are a most desirable creature, you are –
**Alice**: Sir! You should not address me thus! It is not seemly.
**Squire**: Now listen carefully to what I have to say to you. I doubt very much if your wretched sailor husband will return to you and so I –
**Alice**: Say not so! Do not utter such a falsehood! You know not what you say. It could not be true.
**Squire**: Oh, but it is, I tell you. Without doubt, the temptations of foreign parts have proved too much for him. I would not be at all surprised to learn that he has fallen under the spell of one of those no-good dusky maidens who dwell in tropical climes. I am told that they know not the meaning of morality and that every sailor who visits those islands becomes a victim of their shameful advances.
**Alice**: How can you find it in your heart to say such wicked, wicked things? My Tom is a good man. He promised me that he would be faithful and true. He promised that he would think only of me even though oceans divided us.
**Squire**: Ha! Ha! Ha! A likely story indeed. That is what they all say until they set foot upon a foreign shore. Mark my words, he thinks no more of you. He does not give you a second thought. He thinks only of the dark-eyed beauty who dotes upon him and ministers to his every need and desire. He will not return to you – of that you may be certain. He is with another. You have been deserted for ever, usurped by a native charmer.
**Alice**: May Heaven forbid that it be so! May Heaven forbid it!
**Squire**: Think no more of him. Cast him from your thoughts.
**Alice**: If it be true, I am lost for ever. What shall be my fate?

**Squire**: (*aside*) Now, have I gained the advantage; she begins to believe me. Now, will I press my suit. (*aloud*) Never fear, your future is assured. I will look after you. You have but to say the word and I will treat you as you deserve.
**Alice**: (*aside*) Whatever can he mean? (*aloud*) What mean you, sir? I fail to comprehend your intentions.
**Squire**: I thought that I had made my intentions clear enough. Very well then, I will have to show you then, won't I? Come to me, my beauty! (*puts his arm around her*) Come to my arms, my dear.
**Alice**: (*aside*) Alas, I am undone! I am undone! (*aloud*) Unhand me, sir! Unhand me, I say!
**Squire**: Never! Never! You will be mine, mine to do with as I please. (*aside*) Now is my passion roused and I desire most earnestly to possess her.
**Alice**: (*struggling to free herself – aside*) Now must I summon up all my strength if I am to free myself from the clutches of this vile monster who is bent upon taking advantage of me. (*aloud*) Desist, sir, desist! You shall not have your way with me! (*struggles free*).
**Squire**: (*aside*) Ah, I like wenches with spirit. They stir me. (*aloud*) I will treat you like a queen. I will buy you jewels. I will –
**Alice**: I want not your jewels.
**Squire**: Diamonds, emeralds, rubies – all shall be yours.
**Alice**: I want not rubies.
**Squire**: I will dress you in the finest silk. You will be society's pearl. The world shall be your oyster. You shall want for nothing.
**Alice**: Tempt me not, villain! I am not to be bought. Forget not that I am a married woman.
**Squire**: (*catching hold of her again*) Tis useless to resist. You shall be mine, I say – mine!
**Alice**: Never, I would rather die! (*aside*) Heaven support me in my hour of need! Steel my arm to battle for my honour! (*struggles with* SQUIRE *and frees herself*).
**Squire**: (*straightening his coat and moving to centre stage*) Very well! Very well! If that is the way you want it. Do not say that I did not make you the most generous of offers. I promised you much but you saw fit to spurn my advances and so you have only yourself to blame when you finish up in the gutter, where you so rightly belong.
**Alice**: (*moving to right of* SQUIRE) What mean you by that remark?
**Squire**: I would have been good to you. You would have had no need to worry about the rent ever again.

**Alice**: And now what? What mean you?
**Squire**: You see that door – my door?
**Alice**: Yes, I see it.
**Squire**: Out you go, through that door at twelve noon exactly on the last day of this very month. I will not permit you to stay one minute, not one second longer. That is my final word on the matter.
**Alice**: (*on her knees*) Squire Meadows, have pity on me! See, I plead with you on my knees. It is not for my own sake that I plead for mercy. I plead for the sake of my little Mary – the sweetest child who ever drew breath. I plead for the sake of my poor, poor brother, Joe who is so sorely afflicted and could not fend for himself in this wicked, wicked world. I plead for the sake –
**Squire**: Get up, woman! Get up! Cease this pleading nonsense (*going to her*) Tis in vain. You cooked your goose but a minute since when you saw fit to insult me by spurning my generous offers. You will quit this place as I say. I will not be swayed by a weeping woman, grovelling on her knees.
**Alice**: (*crying aloud*) Mercy! Mercy, I say! Mercy! (*grasps his ankles*).
**Squire**: Off, woman, off I say! (*moves away left slightly with* ALICE *still grasping his ankles*) Will you be off! (*throws her to the ground*).

*Enter* JOE *from right, running.*

**Joe**: (*aside*) What be this, then? What be the Squire doing to my dear sister? I will to the rescue. (*aloud*) Leave her be! Just 'ee take thy evil paws off my dear sister or I'll thrash 'ee within an inch of thy wicked life, that I will. (*runs to left of* SQUIRE *and puts up his fists*) Have at 'ee, sir! Have at 'ee! (*aside*) That tells he where he gets off, I reckons.
**Squire**: So, you would threaten me, would you, dog? You would raise your fists to me, eh? How dare you? I'll show you who is the master in these parts (*raises riding crop*). Off, scum! Off, you half-witted lunatic or I'll give you the thrashing you deserve.
**Joe**: (*cowering*) Don't 'ee hit I! Don't 'ee hit I!
**Squire**: Ha! Ha! Ha! Not such a hero now, eh? Now who triumphs? (*still with riding crop raised*).

MARY *and* MRS. BENTLEY *enter right.* MARY *is carrying a basket of food. They move to right centre.*

**Mary**: Look, Mother, what the kind Mrs. Bentley has given us so that we do not starve. Is she not – (*sees* ALICE *lying on the floor – In a matter of fact manner*) Mother, why are you lying on the floor?

**Mrs. B**: (*aside*) Merciful Heaven, what is happening? Why is Squire Meadows threatening poor Joe with his riding crop? Whatever can Joe have done to warrant this attack?
**Mary**: Are you feeling tired, Mother? Why do you not go to bed? They do say that sleep after toil does greatly please.
**Squire**: (*turning from* JOE *who moves down left*) Ah, Mrs. Bentley, is it not? Mrs. Bentley who lives in Lilac Cottage? Your arrival upon the scene is most opportune. You can bear witness to what I am about to say to this woman here. Then, if she is in any doubt whatsoever as to the meaning of my words, you can explain them to her after my departure.
**Alice**: (*rising*) I know not what you have to say to me but nothing can be worse than that which you have already said. I beg of you to hear me and to—
**Squire**: Enough! Enough! (*aside*) This nonsense has gone on long enough. I have never heard so much rubbish in all my life. We are getting nowhere. (*aloud*) I will not listen to another word that issues from your foolish lips. Now then, mark me and mark me well.
**Joe**: (*aside*) I'd mark he for sure if I had my way.
**Squire**: But a moment since, your idiot brother here saw fit to threaten me. As you know, I am not a man to be trifled with. I have been kind and considerate to you, beyond any call of duty, but my patience has been stretched past endurance. Very soon I will start to get angry. I have only one more thing to say to you. Go—pack your bags this instant! You will not stay until the end of the month. I withdraw my bounteous offer.
**Alice**: You cannot mean it!
**Squire**: Indeed I do. I will give you one hour to quit this dwelling, sixty minutes to vacate these premises. If, by then, you have not departed I will call my men and have you thrown out—you and all your miserable belongings.
**Alice**: No! No! Please, listen to me! I would do anything, anything to make you change your mind.
**Squire**: Too late—too late! Go!
**Joe**: (*running to* SQUIRE) Villain! Black-hearted villain! Scurvy, scurrilous seducer!
**Mary**: (*running across to* ALICE *who puts her arms around her*) Mother, mother, do not give way to despair. They do say that despair has power to kill.
**Joe**: I'll make 'ee into mincemeat, that I will.
**Squire**: (*to* JOE) So! So! You would threaten me again, eh? eh? Have at you then! (*starts to thrash* JOE *with his riding crop*).

**Joe**: Stop it! Stop it! Don't 'ee hit I. I be sorry. I gives in. Oh, I be an awful coward, that I be.
**Mary**: He who fights and runs away, may live to fight another day. But he, who in the battle's slain, will never live to fight again.

ALICE *rushes at* SQUIRE *and tries to drag him away from* JOE. MARY *assists.*

**Squire**: Take that—and that—and that!

TOM *rushes in from right. He is dressed as a sailor. He carries a duffle bag. He attacks* SQUIRE *and there is a fight which ends with the* SQUIRE *lying on the floor with* TOM *standing with one foot on the* SQUIRE'S *chest.* (*For the most amusing effect, the fight should only last a second or two*).

**Alice**: Tom! Tom! (*aside*) It is Tom, my sailor husband returned from far-away places across the oceans of the world. Tom, my dear husband whom I feared I might never set eyes upon again in this life. (*aloud*) Tom, you have arrived in the nick of time.
**Mary**: Father, dear Father—home at last (*aside*) Did I not say he would return 'ere long? Do they not say that everything comes to he who waits?
**Tom**: (*gathering* ALICE *and* MARY *into his arms—one on each side*) Alice, my dear wife! Mary, my dear little daughter! How you have grown! Mrs. Bentley, our dear, dear neighbour!
**Alice**: You have returned!
**Mary**: You have returned!
**Mrs. B**: You have returned!
**All**: (*including* SQUIRE) He has returned!
**Tom**: I have returned, never more to sail the seven seas, never more to be parted from my loved ones. But more of that later for now, my beloved wife, there is something I have to tell you.
**Alice**: Yes, husband, yes?
**Tom**: I cannot wait a moment longer.
**Squire**: (*aside*) I'm not surprised.
**Alice**: Tell us, dearest Tom.
**Tom**: There is something I got when I was on the other side of the world.
**Squire**: (*aside*) Just as I said.
**Alice**: Yes? Tell us dear husband.
**Tom**: Can you not guess?
**Squire**: (*aside*) I've got a good idea.
**Mary**:
**Alice**: } No! No! Tell us, tell us what you have got!
**Mrs. B**:

**Tom**: A fortune! I have made my fortune in foreign climes. Our ship was wrecked on a tropical island where we sweltered under a merciless sun for more than three years. We gave up all hope of rescue. That is why I have not communicated with you in all these long years. Whilst we were there, we discovered a pirate's lair.
**Alice**: A pirate's lair?
**Tom**: And in it –
**Alice**: What? What?
**Tom**: Gold! Gold beyond the belief of man.
**Alice**: Gold!
**Squire**: Gold!
**Tom**: Yes, gold. Then one day, a boat bound for Tahiti, hove into our view, we hailed it and it pulled into shore. And so we were rescued at last and set sail for England's shores. Now am I returned to share my fortune with my loving wife, my sweet little daughter and all my beloved family and honest neighbours.
**Alice**: I cannot believe it! I cannot believe it! Tell me then, can we now pay the rent?
**Tom**: Pay the rent?
**Mary**: Do we not have to leave the cottage after all?
**Tom**: Pay the rent! Leave the cottage! There is enough gold in this bag to pay the rent a thousandfold. (*the* SQUIRE *tries to grab the bag but is put down by* TOM'S *foot*).
**Mary**: Oh, Father, do they not say that out of debt is out of danger?
**Tom**: The villain has no hold over us now. We can live in peace for the rest of our days. Dearest wife, from this day forward, all your troubles will be but little ones.
**Mary**: They do say that there are no gains without pains, honesty is the best policy and all's well that ends well.
**Mrs. B**: They do indeed. They do indeed.
**Alice**: Thanks be to Heaven! Thanks be to Heaven!
**All**: Amen! Amen!

CURTAIN

# THE DRUNKARD'S WIFE

*or*

# THE TABLES TURNED

A Melodrama In One Act

*Characters:*

WILLIE BELL (A drunken husband)

MILLIE BELL (His long-suffering wife)

MRS. FERNWAY (An elderly widow woman)

SIR EUSTACE MAKEPEACE (A base, cold-hearted villain)

## THE DRUNKARD'S WIFE *or* THE TABLES TURNED

The setting is the kitchen of a farm labourer's cottage in a small village in Worcestershire. The time 1890 – or what you will.

There is a kitchen table centre stage with a chair on each side. A rocking-chair stands down left. There is a cut-out of a window up-stage centre with the curtains closed. A small table stands left of it. An exit is imagined (behind a flat) up right.

*It is evening and the lighting is fairly dim.* (*Once the effect has been established, the lights could be brought up very slowly to prevent having to play in semi-darkness*). *Mrs. Fernway is in the rocking-chair down left. Her daughter, Millie, is seated right of the table sewing by the light of an oil lamp on the table. Millie stops sewing for a moment and rubs her eyes.*

**Mrs. F**: Tis time you ceased that sewing for this night, my child. You will ruin your eyesight. Have I not told you so these many times?

**Millie**: Alas, I must not cease my labours. Last night 'twas the small hours before I laid down my needle and dragged myself to my bed.

**Mrs. F**: You will make yourself ill and what will become of us then?

**Millie**: But, Mother, you know only too well that the few pitiful pennies which I earn by sewing these shrouds are all that stand between us and starvation. I must not slacken my efforts. How else could we keep body and soul together?

**Mrs. F**: Alackaday! Tis true. Tis only too true. Have I not been a poor widow woman these past twenty years and do I not know that a woman's work is never done? Never!

**Millie**: You have suffered much. I will not attempt to comfort you. Words would be in vain.

**Mrs. F**: Tis I who should comfort you. Have you not a husband who has fallen victim to the demon drink?

**Millie**: Hush, Mother! Say not that. My Willie is not a bad man.

**Mrs. F**: How can you say that? Not one stroke of work has he carried out these past twelve months. Not one penny has he earned to support his young wife – is that not so?

**Millie**: Alas yes – 'tis true.

**Mrs. F**: What of his golden-haired child, who sleeps the sleep of the innocent, in yonder room? Has he done aught to provide for her?
**Millie**: I cannot, in truth, say that he has.
**Mrs. F**: Or his poor old mother-in-law who is so crippled with rheumatics that she can scarce drag one foot after the other? What of her?
**Millie**: Tis but a temporary lapse. If he could but find employment again, he would reform. Of that I am certain. Once more would his noble feet tread the straight and narrow path of sobriety.
**Mrs. F**: Do not deceive yourself, my child. His lips have tasted the evil drink.
**Millie**: Ah me!
**Mrs. F**: He is a slave of the beast.
**Millie**: Woe is me!
**Mrs. F**: He has been plunged into dissipation!
**Millie**: Alas! Alas!
**Mrs. F**: He is a devotee of Bacchus!
**Millie**: That as well?
**Mrs. F**: Did not your father, God rest his soul, follow the same path? Did he not drink himself into an early grave? Did he not leave me with a young one to raise without assistance from man or parish? (*starts to cry*).

**Millie**: (*rising and crossing in front of table to right of* MRS. FERNWAY) Now, now, Mother do not lacerate your heart so.

**Mrs. F**: To think that my child, whom I nursed and cared for all those years, through trials and tribulations should wed a man who, like her poor father, cannot resist the temptation of the bottle. (*sobs*).

**Millie**: Hush, Mother, hush! He is a good man at heart. He has but been led astray. He will reform 'ere long—fear not.
**Mrs. F**: Where is he now, then? Tell me that. When did you last see your Willie? Whose hard-earned money is he pouring away down at the ale house? Money which my poor daughter earned by the sweat of her brow—earned by working her fingers to the bone and her beautiful blue eyes until they have turned red with the strain and fatigue? He has brought disgrace to this household.

**Millie**: (*looking out front*) The name of my husband is not lost even though it be coupled with that of—of—

**Mrs. F**: Drunkard! Why do you not say the word? A drunkard he is and a drunkard he will remain.

**Millie**: (*moving away to centre stage below table – aside*) I will speak to him when he returns. Once more, will I beg him to realise the error of his ways.
**Mrs. F**: (*rising*) Give me my stick!
**Millie**: (*turning to* MRS. FERNWAY) Your stick? Why do you want your stick?
**Mrs. F**: I am going out.
**Millie**: Whither go you?
**Mrs. F**: To the village.
**Millie**: But 'tis past nine of the clock. Where can you possibly be going at this hour?
**Mrs. F**: That is my business. I refuse to impart that knowledge to you. Tis my concern and mine alone.
**Millie**: Oh, Mother! (*goes to right of* MRS. FERNWAY).
**Mrs. F**: Do not trouble yourself. Darkly shadowed is the sky that hangs gloomily over your young head. Better you should not know.
**Millie**: (*putting her arms around* MRS. FERNWAY) But, Mother dearest, dearest mother of mine, 'tis a fearful night. Tis bitter cold and the snow lies thick upon the ground, 'twould freeze your old bones. Tell me, Mother, tell me the purpose of your intended nocturnal peregrination!
**Mrs. F**: Very well, child, very well. I will tell you as I perceive only too well that you are bent on discovering the reason why I am determined to absent myself from this abode for a while.
**Millie**: Yes, yes?
**Mrs. F**: I go – to the ale house!

**Millie**: Oh no, Mother – not you also!

**Mrs. F**: To the ale house. There will I apprehend your inebrious husband. There will I objurgate him and bring him home to his dolorous spouse.

**Millie**: Mother, you know not what you say! You are overwrought. It must not be.

**Mrs. F**: Give me my stick, girl!

**Millie**: (*fetching stick from left side of table and taking it to* MRS. FERNWAY) Very well, Mother – here is your stick. But, for the final time, let me beseech you not to venture out into the cold, cold snow – not in your condition.

**Mrs. F**: (*pushing past* MILLIE *and hobbling to right of centre table*) Out of my way, child. Tis time a body spoke their mind in this house (*to door and turning*) I will seek out your drunken husband and return him to the bosom of his family, even if it is my last act upon this earth. (*exit up right*).

**Millie**: (*calling*) Mother! Mother! Come back! Come back! (*runs up to exit*) Mother! Mother! (*after a pause returns to chair right of table and sinks into it and, with her head in her hands, cries bitterly*) Heaven save me! Heaven save me!

*A knock at the door.* MILLIE *rises.*

**Millie**: Ah! Tis Mother! She has returned already. (*another knock*) But 'tis strange that she should knock. Ah! Perhaps 'tis not she! (*another knock*) I will go to the door to ascertain the identity of the caller at so late an hour. (*goes to door and opens it partly*) Is that you, Mother? Mother? Can you hear me? Is that you? (*stands back*) 'Tis not Mother. 'Tis another. 'Tis Sir Eustace Makepeace who lives up at the Hall. Whatever can he want at this hour?

**Sir E**: (*off*) Don't be frightened, my dear. Tis I – Sir Eustace Makepeace. May I come inside for a moment or two?

**Millie**: Why, Sir Eustace, we are indeed honoured that you should wish to visit us in our humble abode.

**Sir R**: (*off*) May I come in? Tis cold outside.

**Millie**: (*opening door*) Enter! Enter. You are most welcome.

SIR EUSTACE *enters, shaking off the snow. He moves to right of centre table.* MILLIE *moves to table and scoops up all the sewing and stands above the table.*

**Millie**: Sir Eustace, won't you sit down, please?

**Sir E**: (*sitting right of table*) Thank you, my dear. You are most kind. If I may be permitted to say so, as kind as you are beautiful. (*aside*) Egad, this wench stirs me (*aloud*) – very beautiful.

**Millie**: Sir Eustace, you flatter! It is not right you should say these things to a young woman such as I. (*moves upstage and puts sewing on table left of window*).

**Sir E**: Egad, and why not if they are true? Eh? Eh?

MILLIE *moves to left of centre table.*

**Sir E**: (*leaning across table to* MILLIE) Tell me, girl, are we alone in this house? Eh? Eh?

**Millie**: My beloved child lies in yonder room, wrapped in the arms of slumber.

**Sir E**: Asleep, eh? And your old mother – where is she?

**Millie**: She has stepped out for a moment. I am expecting her return 'ere long.

**Sir E**: I see. I see. Good! (*aside*) Curse the woman, I thought she would be absent longer. (*aloud*) Now, I imagine that you are wondering why I called to see you so late at night – eh? eh?

**Millie**: Indeed yes. I cannot imagine what you want with me.

**Sir E**: (*aside*) But I can. I know only too well. Ha! Ha! Ha!

(*aloud*) Do sit down, my dear. That way I will feel more at home, don't you know?
**Millie**: Very well, if you insist. Thank you, Sir Eustace. (*sits left of table*).
**Sir E**: Good! Good! Now then—are you sitting comfortably? Good! Then I'll begin. Now, you know me, I'm a man who doesn't mince words—if you take my meaning. I'll come directly to the point.
**Millie**: Yes! Yes!
**Sir E**: I have called to see you about your no-good husband.
**Millie**: My husband! What of him?
**Sir E**: It is with the deepest regret that I have to tell you . .
**Millie**: (*rising*) He has had an accident? He has collided with a cart?
**Sir E**: No! No!
**Millie**: Hit by a horse?
**Sir E**: No! No!
**Millie**: Battered by a bull?
**Sir E**: No! No! No! Nothing like that. He is not injured in any way.
**Millie**: What then?
**Sir E**: Sit down, my dear and calm yourself and I will tell you.
**Millie**: (*sitting*) Very well.
**Sir E**: He is in trouble—very serious trouble.
**Millie**: My Willie in trouble? What is the nature of the trouble?
**Sir E**: I find it most painful to be the bearer of such tidings.
**Millie**: Go on.
**Sir E**: Certain valuable items of jewellery are missing from The Gables.
**Millie**: Items of jewellery? But what can that possibly have to do with my Willie?
**Sir E**: I will tell you. Are you acquainted with old Mr. Peabody who lives in the cottage hard by the lodge?
**Millie**: Old Mr. Peabody? I have seen him often enough but know him not to speak to.
**Sir E**: Ah! Well, on the night of the robbery, old Mr. Peabody was standing at the door of his cottage, taking in the night air. What do you think he saw?
**Millie**: What? Tell me!
**Sir E**: He saw—and he is prepared to so swear in a court of law if necessity has it—he saw your husband.
**Millie**: My husband!
**Sir E**: Yes, your husband. He was proceeding down the drive of The Gables at about 11 of the clock. He was

carrying a small brown bag. Old Mr. Peabody says that your husband was in an advanced state of intoxication and that he stumbled and fell, just as he approached the gates.
**Millie**: (*aside*) My poor, dear Willie!
**Sir E**: As he fell, in his drunkard stupor, the bag he was carrying opened and several items of jewellery fell out.
**Millie**: But he must be mistaken. My Willie would not be the perpetrator of such a dastardly deed.
**Sir E**: No mistake, I assure you. Alas, no mistake. In his obfuscation, he failed to notice a ring which had rolled across the drive. When old Mr. Peabody called "Stop, thief!", your husband scooped up the rest of the trinkets, returned them to the reticule and absquatulated, abandoning the irrefutable evidence of his malfeasance.
**Millie**: (*aside*) Alas, 'tis all too clear.
**Sir E**: Old Mr. Peabody showed me the ring to which I have just referred. He showed it to me the very next day. There can be no doubt about it—no doubt whatsoever. It was one of Sir Hector's rings. It has his initials engraved upon it. What is more, old Mr. Peabody swears he could positively identify your husband as the rapscallion he beheld that night.
**Millie**: (*rising and moving down left—aside*) This is terrible, terrible! Whatever shall I do? Whatever shall I do?

**Sir E**: (*aside*) So far my plan proceeds excellently—most excellently. Now for the next stage of my schemes and the undoing of this delectable damzel. (*aloud*) Do not distress yourself, my dear. Do not distress yourself. All is not yet lost.
**Millie**: (*turning*) No?
**Sir E**: (*rising and moving to below centre table*) No, no—of course not. Now—just listen to me and I will outline the plan I have in mind. I have a little proposition to make to you, my dear.
**Millie**: A proposition! (*aside*) Whatever can he mean? I cannot imagine.
**Sir E**: I will elucidate. Old Mr. Peabody tells me that he has acquainted no one but myself with the events of that evening as witnessed by himself.
**Millie**: Yes?
**Sir E**: For several years he was in my employ. During that time he—but we will not pursue that point at present. Suffice it to say that if I advise him that it is in his best interest, he will not divulge the identity of the thief to a living soul. Now—tell me, do you think that I should tell old Mr. Peabody to hold his peace? Eh? Eh?

**Millie**: Could you? Would you?
**Sir E**: Certainly I would, my dear. Certainly.
**Millie**: (*moving to left of* SIR EUSTACE) Oh, Sir Eustace. I would I could die at your feet.
**Sir E**: (*aside*) That's not exactly what I had in mind.
**Millie**: Words cannot describe the joy I feel. I never doubted the goodness of your heart. You are kindness itself.
**Sir E**: Nay! Nay! Tis nothing.
**Millie**: Your benevolent benignity is only exceeded by your salubrious, salutary saintliness.
**Sir E**: Nay! Nay! Nay! You o'erwhelm me.
**Millie**: Bless you, Sir Eustace—bless you!
**Sir E**: There is however one condition appertaining to my vow of silence.
**Millie**: But name it, dear sir. But name it.
**Sir E**: (*aside*) Now am I indeed in sight of my goal. (*aloud*) Well, as I may have said before, I do not believe in beating about the bush. I—I—I
**Millie**: Sir, sir—why do you hesitate? Out with it! Out with it this very minute.
**Sir E**: Very well. I have long been an admirer of your beauty.
**Millie**: My beauty? What mean you?
**Sir E**: I will speak plainly. I am tantalized by your pulchritudinous splendiferous sublimity.
**Millie**: (*aside*) Ah—now I perceive his meaning (*aloud moving left*) Sir, you forget you are a gentleman. I am a married woman.
**Sir E**: Your wretched husband is not worthy of consideration. He has been proved to be a thief and a drunkard. You owe him no further allegiance.
**Millie**: That is not true (*turning*) What is it? What do you want of me?
**Sir E**: All I ask is that you would do me the honour of visiting me from time to time.
**Millie**: Visit you? What do you mean? Where do you wish me to visit you?
**Sir E**: Why, at the Hall of course, my dear. It is a lonely bachelor establishment and I live the life of a trappist monk.
**Millie**: Ah, I see. You require a maidservant. You wish me to serve you.
**Sir E**: No! No! I am but asking you if you would call upon me now and then.
**Millie**: To take tea?
**Sir E**: You shall have tea—yes, indeed you shall. But then—after tea . . .

**Millie**: Yes?
**Sir E**: Perhaps you would condescend to bestow certain favours upon me.
**Millie**: (*turning away—aside*) Do I hear right? Do my ears mock me? (*turning back to* SIR EUSTACE—*aloud*) You cannot mean—you do not mean . . .
**Sir E**: (*twirling his moustache*) Exactly! Exactly! (*going close to* MILLIE) Now I believe we see eye to eye, do we not? I cannot wait for the day. (*puts arm around her*) You arouse my passion. You are the object of my desire. (*turns to kiss her*) Give me a foretaste of the carnal joys to come.
**Millie**: Never! Never! Unhand me, sir! Unhand me or I will call for the officers of the law.
**Sir E**: (*holding her at arms length*) Ha! Ha! Ha! You forget, my proud beauty, you are in my power. It is I who would send for the officers of the law and have your drunken husband flung into prison.
**Millie**: (*beating his chest*) Villain! Scoundrel! Malefactor!
**Sir E**: Ha! Ha! Ha!
**Millie**: Reprobate! Recreant!
**Sir E**: Ha! Ha! Ha!
**Millie**: Misdemeanist! Caitiff!
**Sir E**: Ha! Ha! Ha!
**Millie**: (*aside*) Ah! Words fail me.
**Sir E**: (*pushing her aside and moving to down right of centre table*) Sticks and stones may break my bones . . . You may call me what you will. I have the upper hand (*turning to* MILLIE) You will do my bidding, I promise you. You will dance to my tune.
**Millie**: I—I—but wait. A thought has just occurred to me.
**Sir E**: What mean you?
**Millie**: (*moving to below centre table*) How do I know you speak the truth? Could it be that you are attempting to trick me?
**Sir E**: Trick you?
**Millie**: (*aside*) Is it possible that this is some fallaciousness recounted with the object of forcing me to yield to his rapacious libido? (*aloud*) Sir Eustace, I will speak plainly. I do not believe you!
**Sir E**: Not believe me? You are raving, girl—raving.
**Millie**: I am resolved to put this matter to the test. This very next morning, will I visit old Mr. Peabody at his cottage.
**Sir E**: Visit old Mr. Peabody! (*aside*) Curse the girl! (*aloud*) With what object?
**Millie**: To obtain his confirmation of the events of that

night. To ask him if he did, in fact, see my husband with the stolen jewellery. I have only your word for it and I trust you not, villain!

**Sir E**: (*moving down right*) So! So! I see! (*aside*) Now must I think quickly if I am to retain the advantage I have over this girl. (*aloud—turning to* MILLIE) Very well, very well if that is the way you wish to play the game, so be it. I will away this instant. (*moving right of centre table*).

**Millie**: Whither go you?

**Sir E**: To see old Mr. Peabody and inform him that I have changed my mind. To tell him to go without delay to the local constabulary.

**Millie**: (*running up and catching hold of* SIR EUSTACE) No! No! I beseech you. Do not call on old Mr. Peabody! Have mercy!

**Sir E**: Mercy! Why should I show you mercy?

**Millie**: Tis not for myself alone. Think of my poor old widowed mother. She is not long for this world, I fear. The shame and disgrace would precipitate her demise. Let her die in peace in her own time.

**Sir E**: Enough! I am growing weary of these nonsensical ramblings. I go! (*turns*).

**Millie**: (*catching hold of him*) Hold, I say! You shall hear me. In yonder room lies a young, innocent child. Her golden locks are spread upon her pillow. As yet, she is unaware of the ways of the world. She is all that we have in this life. What will become of her if her father is sent to prison as a common thief?

**Sir E**: He should have considered that before he committed the crime (*pushing her aside*) Now, out of my way. I will hear no more. (*to door—turning*) When your disreputable husband has been brought to trial, condemned and sentenced to imprisonment or transportation to Australia, remember that you were given the opportunity to save him from such a fate. Remember that, girl! (*exit*).

*When he has gone,* MILLIE *staggers to below table.*

**Millie**: Heaven support me in my hour of trial. (*sinking to ground*) Whatever shall I do? (*out front*) Perhaps I should reconsider his proposition. Should I? Perhaps I should surrender myself to the villain for the sake of my family. Should I? Perhaps I should quaff the bitter cup of self-sacrifice. Should I? Should I? (*rising*) No! No! No! Never! Never! Never! I could not submit to the desires of that foul monster. His insalubrious encinctures would stifle me with their squadility. I am resolved! But if what he says is indeed true, then will he instruct old Mr. Peabody to acquaint the officers of the law. Then will all be lost—lost—lost.

(*A knock at the door*).

Another visitor? (*starting back*) Ah, could it be the officers of the law already? Have they come to arrest my poor Willie? (*another knock*) I must answer. I have no alternative but to do so. (*goes to door*) Who is it? Who is without? What want you at this hour?

**Voice**: (*off—feeble*) It is I—old Mr. Peabody. Can I come inside for a moment? The snow is falling fast and I am very, very cold.

**Millie**: (*aside*) Old Mr. Peabody, here? (*aloud*) But a moment and I'll let you in.

*She opens the door and lets in old* MR. PEABODY (*who, in fact is* SIR EUSTACE *disguised with a white wig and a long white beard. He walks bent almost double*).

**Mr. P**: Thank you, my dear. You are most kind. May I sit down for an instant? I am very old and my feeble limbs will scarce even support the weight of my poor, frail body.

**Millie**: But of course. Permit me to give you a hand. (*leads him to chair right of centre table where he sits. She moves behind table to chair left and sits*).

**Mr. P**: Thank you, my dear. Your consideration for an old man is most welcome. (*aside*) Little does she know 'tis I—Sir Eustace Makepeace in disguise. Ha! Ha! Ha! (*aloud*) Now, my dear I do not wish to take up much of your time. I'm sure you are anxious to learn the reason for my visit, so I will out with it, without further delay.

**Millie**: Yes!

**Mr. P**: I was on my way home, but a moment since, battling against the cruel snow, when I saw Sir Eustace Makepeace leaving this very cottage. He acquainted me with the knowledge of that which had befallen within these walls. He adjured me to visit you to confirm his report of that which I had witnessed the other night.

**Millie**: And you confirm it?

**Mr. P**: Alas, yes.

**Millie**: Then 'tis true! Tis true!

**Mr. P**: As true as my name is Peabody. It is most sad, most sad. But you have no cause for alarm. Sir Eustace explained to me that it would serve my interest ill if I were to reveal all. You see, several years ago, I was foolish enough to—to . . . but never mind that now; suffice it to say that the kind, noble Sir Eustace rescued me from an ignominious situation. If he asks me to remain silent, you may rest assured that my lips will be sealed for ever.

**Millie**: Do you, indeed, promise that?
**Mr. P**: Of a certainty.
**Millie**: (*rising and moving behind table to up right of* MR. P) How can I ever repay you? Your courteous act will not go unrewarded (MR. PEABODY *turns to her*)—in Heaven.
**Mr. P**: (*aside*) But I cannot wait until then to ravish the girl. I am resolved to possess her without further delay. (*aloud*) Sir Eustace instructed me to inform you that, now that you know beyond a shadow of doubt of your husband's guilt, he expects you to reconsider the decision you made when he was here earlier this evening. He said that you would know exactly what he means.
**Millie**: (*moving to behind table—aside*) That I do, only too well. (*aloud—turning to* MR. PEABODY) And did he say what the outcome would be if I heeded not his request?
**Mr. P**: He told me to tell you that if you were foolish enough to refuse his offer, you would live to rue the day you spurned him.
**Millie**: (*aside*) I am a virtuous woman. I refuse to betray my husband with that snake in the grass, with that viper in the bosom, with that foul, cheating, hypocritical, blackguardly limb of Satan. (*aloud*) Tell him, I'd rather not.
**Mr. P**: Very well, if that's the way you want it, I'll tell him.
**Millie**: Tell him also that I would rather die. Tell him he shall not have his way. Tell him I am resolved.
**Mr. P**: (*rising and hobbling back to door—aside, as* SIR EUSTACE) Stupid girl. She knows not what she does. But I still have one plan left to ensnare her. She will not escape this one. Ha! Ha! Ha! (*aloud*) Goodnight, girl, I will convey your sentiments to Sir Eustace. Never fear! (*exit*).
**Millie**: (*aside*) Heaven alone knows what is in store for me. What now shall be my course of action? Old Mr. Peabody confirms the words of Sir Eustace (*moving above table to left of left chair*) Oh, merciful Heaven, protect me and show me what I should do now in my terrible predicament. If I refuse the odious advances of this devil in human shape, he will hand my dear Willie over to the officers of the law. If I succumb to the advances of that beast I—I . . . . but 'tis too awful to contemplate, too unspeakable to countenance. (*knock at door—loud*) Yet another knock! Who can it be this time? (*goes to door*) Who are you? (*pause*) Answer, I charge you!
**Voice**: (*off*) Open in the name of the law!
**Millie**: (*aside*) Could it be an officer of the law? (*aloud*) Who are you, I say? Answer!
**Voice**: (*off*) Constable Miller. Open this door at once or I

will be obliged to break it down.
**Millie**: Constable Miller!
**Voice**: (*off*) That is correct. Open this door, in the name of the law.
**Millie**: (*aside*) He has come to arrest my poor Willie. (*aloud*) I'm opening the door.

*She opens the door and a police officer enters* (*in fact, it is* SIR EUSTACE *now disguised as an officer of the law. He now sports a black moustache and a black beard*).

**Con. M**: I am Constable Miller. (*aside*) But I am really Sir Eustace Makepeace. The stupid girl will not see through my disguise, I warrant. (*aloud*) Are you Mrs. William Bell?
**Millie**: I am indeed. I would not wish to deny it. (*moving to below table*).
**Con. M**: (*to her right*) If you please, ma'am, it's your husband I wish to see. It is necessary that I have a few words with him with the minimum of delay.
**Millie**: He is not here. Could you not return in the morning?
**Con. M**: I'm very sorry, ma'am, but that is impossible—quite impossible. I wish to speak with your husband on a matter of great import. Are you cognizant of his whereabouts?
**Millie**: (*aside*) I fear I am indeed. (*aloud*) I think I know where he is. I cannot tell a lie.
**Con. M**: Exactly, exactly. I was proceeding along the High Street in a northerly direction but five minutes since. When I drew level with the ale house, I happened to glance through the window of the public bar. What do you think I saw there, eh?
**Millie**: (*aside*) Shame! Shame! That it should come to this! (*aloud*) What did you see? Tell me.
**Con. M**: Can you not guess?
**Millie**: My poor Willie?
**Con. M**: Exactly, exactly. He was, I regret to inform you, as drunk as David's sow. He could scarce stand. Two of his besotted companions were supporting him. He was shouting abuse.
**Millie**: My Willie does not shout abuse!
**Con. M**: Oh but he was, ma'am. Shouting at all and sundry in a slurred, inebriated voice. Never before have I seen such a bibulous, bibacious, befuddled blighter.
**Millie**: (*aside*) He must have been drinking again. (*aloud*) I am certain you are mistaken.
**Con. M**: No mistake. As I say, he was shouting at the top of his voice.
**Millie**: Perhaps he was asking someone to open a window.

Perhaps he was overcome by the heat of the ale house and was feeling faint.
**Con. M**: I believe it to be otherwise.
**Millie**: What did you do then?
**Con. M**: Nothing. I considered the matter for a moment and decided that he was not disturbing the peace outside the ale house. Besides, at that time, I was not in possession of the full facts. I was not aware of the circumstances. I had no cause to interfere.
**Millie**: What circumstances?
**Con. M**: All in good time. All in good time. Passing on my way, who should I happen to meet but old Mr. Peabody coming down the lane from the direction of this cottage.
**Millie**: (*aside*) Old Mr. Peabody!! (*aloud*) Old Mr. Peabody?
**Con. M**: "Constable Miller" says he, "I have something of import with which to acquaint you". "Have you, indeed?" says I. "That I have" says he.
**Millie**: Yes? Yes?
**Con. M**: Do you know what it was he told me, Mrs. Bell?
**Millie** (*aside—moving away left*) Only too well—only too well. (*turning*) Tell me, Constable Miller. Tell me.
**Con. M**: (*aside*) She sees not through my disguise. What is more she grows anxious. I'll have her soon, I swear—Ha! Ha! Ha! (*aloud, going to right of* MILLIE) Where was your husband, William Bell, on the evening of Tuesday 22nd January last between 10.30 and 11.30 p.m.?
**Millie**: Between 10.30 and 11.30?
**Con. M**: That is what I said.
**Millie**: I cannot rightly say.
**Con. M**: (*moving back to centre below table*) Tis of no consequence. I will ask him that question himself when he returns, providing he is in any fit state to answer.
**Millie**: But I know not when he will return.
**Con. M**: Then I'll wait here until he does, even if I have to wait all night.
**Millie**: (*crossing to left of* CONSTABLE MILLER, *kneeling and catching hold of him*) For mercy's sake, I ask you to forbear! Have pity on us, I implore you! Have pity! We have always been law-abiding folk. It was the demon drink which affected his reasoning. He knew not what he did!
**Con. M**: Get up, woman, (*she rises*) What was that you said just now? Say it once more.
**Millie**: (*kneeling as before*) For mercy's sake, I ask you to forbear—
**Con. M**: No—not all of it—just the last part.

**Millie**: (*rising*) He knew not what he did.
**Con. M**: I thought that's what you said. So—you do know aught of what occurred that night, eh? (*aside*) Out of her own mouth has the girl betrayed herself—I will press the point (*aloud*) I repeat—you know aught of what occurred that night—eh?
**Millie** (*aside*) What did I say? I am undone! (*aloud*) Have pity, I say! I am a good woman.
**Con. M**: (*aside*) But not for much longer if my plan succeeds —oh no—not for much longer. Ha! Ha! Ha! (*aloud*) Now girl, it would appear that—(*there is a noise outside*).
**Con. M**: There is a noise outside. Doubtless it is your drunken husband staggering up the pathway to the cottage door.
**Millie**: (*aside*) I must warn him. I must warn him. I will run out and tell him to flee (*pushing past* CONSTABLE MILLER *and running to door*).
**Con. M**: (*turning*) Where are you going?
**Millie**: I want to go outside. I need to go outside.

*At that monent*, MRS. FERNWAY *enters*. MILLIE *starts back to above chair right of table.*

**Millie**: Mother!
**Mrs. F**: (*seeing* CONSTABLE MILLER) An officer of the law! (*aside*) What could bring him here so late at night? (*aloud*) What is the officer doing here, Millie? (*moves to right of* MILLIE).
**Millie**: Oh, lackaday! He wants to see my Willie.
**Mrs. F**: Why does he wish to see your Willie?
**Millie**: We are undone! All will be exposed 'ere long.
**Mrs. F**: What mean you, girl? Explain yourself. You are talking in riddles.
**Millie**: He has seen Willie, down at the ale house.
**Mrs. F**: At the ale house? When did he see Willie at the ale house?
**Con. M**: But ten minutes past. He was in an advanced state of intoxication.
**Mrs. F**: (*crossing* MILLIE—*to right of* CONSTABLE MILLER) That is a falsehood!
**Millie**: (*to right of* MRS. FERNWAY) A falsehood?
**Con. M**: A falsehood?
**Mrs. F**: A falsehood, an untruth, an equivocation—a lie!
**Millie**: You mean that he is not telling the truth? You mean that he is telling a fib? Why say you that?
**Mrs. F**: I have just left the ale house. Your husband, Willie, has not stepped over its threshold all evening.
**Millie**: All evening?

ASIDE

**Con. M**: All evening? (*aside*) This is some diabolical plot to outwit me but it will not succeed.
**Mrs. F**: I had it from the lips of the landlord himself, no less. He says he has not seen him at all since last night.
**Millie**: Wherever can he be?
**Mrs. F**: Wherever can he be?
**Con. M**: Wherever can he be?

*The door opens and* WILLIE *enters.*

**Willie**: I am here. I have come back (*stands up right*).
**Millie**: Sober! (*aside*) Heaven be praised.
**Mrs. F**: Sober! (*aside*) Do my eyes and ears deceive me?
ASIDE **Con. M**: Sober! (*aside*) Curse him! He will not outwit me!
**Millie**: (*running to left of* WILLIE) We thought you had been at the ale house. Mother has just returned from there this very moment.
**Willie**: Mother!
**Millie**: Yes, she came to find you and bring you back to your loved ones from that den of iniquity.
**Willie**: That was not necessary. I have not been there.
**Millie**: Where have you been, then?
**Willie**: (*stepping forward*) I have been—
**Millie**:
**Mrs. F**: } Yes?
**Con. M**:
**Willie**: I have been to sign the pledge!
**Millie**: (*coming down to his left*) The pledge?
**Willie**: Never more will foul liquor pass my lips. I have been freed from the terrible curse. Last night I met a poor man even more afflicted than I. He writhed in torment on the floor. He called out that a huge snake was twining itself around him. His brain was on fire, hideous visions appeared before his eyes. In his delirium, he begged us to take off the monster which was devouring him. Twas then I came to realise the error of my ways. If this was to be my future, thought I, then better to be dead—dead—dead! I thought of my dear ones at home and of all the suffering and evil that cling around a drunkard's house. "No more" said I. "No more! Henceforth will I tread the sober path, hand in hand with my long-suffering wife, her old mother and my darling child".
**Millie**: He is saved! He is saved! Thank God!
**Mrs. F**: Amen! Amen! (*sits in chair right of table*).
**Con. M**: (*moving down left—aside*) Curses! Curses! Curses! ASIDE How now shall I proceed if I am to procure the wife of this man?
**Willie**: But what is Constable Miller doing here?

**Millie**: Oh, Willie, Willie! I fear that your reformation may have come too late—too late!
**Willie**: What mean you? (*crossing to right of* CONSTABLE MILLER) What is it you want here?
**Millie**: (*crossing to his right—taking his arm*) Willie, Constable Miller wishes to speak to you about the events of the other evening.
**Willie**: (*turning to her*) The other evening?
**Millie**: Yes, he went down to the ale house earlier tonight to see . . . (*aside*) But what can this mean? (*aloud*) Willie, are you sure you were not at the ale house tonight?
**Willie**: Have I not told you that I went to sign the pledge?
**Millie**: Then how could Constable Miller have seen you there?

**Con. M**: (*aside*) Foiled! Foiled again!
**Willie**: He could not have seen me! (*to* CONSTABLE MILLER) What mean you by this accusation?
**Con. M**: (*aside*) All is not lost. He knows not that I am Sir Eustace Makepeace or that I was old Mr. Peabody. Now must I proceed with caution if I am to gain the day. (*aloud*) I—I—
**Willie**: Come, sir. I await your answer.
**Con. M**: I—I—
**Willie**: Yes? Come, sir (*grabbing hold of him*) Why indulge in these falsehoods?
**Con. M**: Lay not your hands on an officer of the law!
**Willie**: I'm not afraid of you. Come—answer my question (*shakes him—his false beard is dislodged*) So! So! You are not Constable Miller after all—eh? Who are you then? (*pulls off the beard*) Sir Eustace Makepeace!
**Mrs. F**: (*rising*) Sir Eustace Makepeace!
**Millie**: Sir Eustace Makepeace!

**Sir E**: (*aside*) I fear I am discovered. (*aloud*) Just a jest—nothing more. Think nothing of it. I'm a terrible joker.
**Willie**: A jest indeed! (*grabbing hold of* SIR EUSTACE *again*) Come, man—tell me the reason for the disguise or I will thrash the living daylight out of you, as sure as my name is William Bell.
**Sir E**: How dare you lay hands on me, you ruffian—you dog? Do you know who I am?
**Willie**: That I do—a rogue and a reprobate, I'll be bound. I ask you again, what was the purpose of your disguise? I demand to know!
**Sir E**: (*aside*) Now for the last trump in my hand. If it fails to take the trick, then am I truly lost. (*aloud*) You think you are a brave man, don't you? Well, let me tell you, you won't be so brave when I go to see old Mr. Peabody and tell him

to go and fetch the officers of the law.
**Willie**: Old Mr. Peabody? What is all this about old Mr. Peabody?
**Millie**: He was here earlier this evening. He had frightful tidings to tell.
**Willie**: Old Mr. Peabody here? But that is impossible!
**Millie**: Impossible? What mean you?
**Sir E**: Yes—what mean you? Speak up man!
**Willie**: Old Mr. Peabody went to Somerset three days ago to see his son and daughter-in-law. He will not return until next week.
**Sir E**: (*aside*) Ah! He has been my undoing! (*aloud*) You are mistaken.
**Willie**: No mistake, I assure you.
**Millie**: Then it can't have been old Mr. Peabody who came here this evening.
**Willie**: Exactly (*turns to* MILLIE).
**Millie**: Then who was it?
**Willie**: I don't think we need to look far to find the answer to that conundrum. I know who it was.

SIR EUSTACE *starts to creep towards the door via upstage of the table.*

**Millie**: You do?
**Mrs. F**: (*standing in his path with stick raised*) It was this rogue here, was it not?

MILLIE *to right of* MRS. FERNWAY. WILLIE *behind table to left of* SIR EUSTACE. MILLIE *to left of centre table.*

**Willie**: Indeed it was, was it not? (*grabs* SIR EUSTACE *shakes him again*) Come on, man—the truth for once in your life.
**Sir E**: Curse you, yes it was I. Stop hurting me! Stop it, I say! I will tell all if you cease this unwarranted assault upon my person.
**Millie**: If old Mr. Peabody went to Somerset three days ago, how could he have seen Willie coming out of The Gables?
**Willie**: Out of The Gables? What do you mean? I have not been near The Gables these twelve months past.
**Millie**: Do you swear that?
**Willie**: I swear it.
**Millie**: Then you did not steal the jewellery?
**Willie**: Steal the jewellery? Whatever do you mean?
**Millie**: Sir Eustace, here, said that old Mr. Peabody saw you coming down the drive of The Gables, the other night, carrying a bag of jewellery.
**Willie**: It is a falsehood! (*to* SIR EUSTACE) So this is another example of your mendacity is it not? Eh? (*twists* SIR EUSTACE'S *arm*).

**Sir E**: Stop! Stop! You are hurting me again. But stop and I will reveal all.
**Willie**: I'll stop when you tell me and not before.
**Sir E**: Curse you! Curse you! Ouch! Ouch! Very well—it was I.
**Willie**: What do you mean, it was you?
**Sir E**: I stole the jewellery.
**Millie**: You?
**Mrs. F**: You?
**Willie**: You? Why?
**Sir E**: I thought that if I could make your wife believe it was you, it would give me a hold over her.
**Willie**: But why, for what reason? Why should you wish to have a hold over my wife? Come, man, I want your answer!
**Sir E**: I—I—(WILLIE *twists his arm again*) I—ouch! I wanted her for myself.
**Willie**: You mean—you can't mean—(*looking at* SIR EUSTACE) You do mean . . . Mother! Go at once and fetch the real Constable Miller and bring him here. Before the church clock strikes the midnight hour this scurvy knave will be where he so rightly belongs—behind bars. Villain, we have witnessed your confession. All is over.
**Mrs. F**: (*to door*) I go to fetch the officers of the law to apprehend this vile man and remove him to where he will receive his just deserts (*exit*).
**Willie**: If ever you cross my path again, I'll level you to the ground and spit upon you as a debased, degraded menial beneath my contempt.
**Sir E**: Now all is truly lost—lost for ever! (*sinks into chair right of table centre*).
**Millie**: (*moving to below table*—WILLIE *moves to her left*) And we are saved! Saved! Never more will we have cause to fear. The vile villain is outwitted and my dear, dear husband has signed the pledge. We are restored, once more, to happiness and we will live in peace from this day forward.
**Willie**: (*his arms around* MILLIE) Praise be to Heaven! Praise be to Heaven!

CURTAIN

# THE GYPSY CURSE

*or*

# THE FLOWER OF THE TRIBE

## A Melodrama In One Act

*Characters*

ISHMAEL LEE (The head of the gypsy tribe)
MEG LEE (His wife)
NELL HATFIELD (Their widowed daughter)
ZELLA LEE (Their younger daughter)
PHAROS LEE (Their son)
WILLIAM CORDER (The Squire's son – a villain)

# THE GYPSY SONG

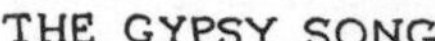

Repeat chorus after final verse.

# THE GYPSY CURSE *or* THE FLOWER OF THE TRIBE

The setting is a gypsy encampment on the edge of a wood in Polstead, Suffolk in the early 1820s. Part of a tent can be seen stage left. There is a 'cut-out' tree up right and another up centre. There is a tree stump down right centre. A camp fire is alight centre stage.

*When the curtain rises, the gypsies are seated round the camp fire. Ishmael upstage of the fire with Meg on his right and Nell on his left. Pharos is right of Meg and Zella left of Nell. They are singing.*

**Gypsies**: Oh, who so free as the gypsy race?
We sleep in the frost and snow.
No roof we need but the sky above.
Our couch is the turf below.
Then hey, fal de ral! Who so free?
Oh, the gypsy's roving life for me.

We strike our tents at the close of day,
Then off to another town,
For no cause have we to further stay
When stalls at the fair are down.
Then hey, fal de ral! Who so free?
Oh, the gypsy's roving life for me.

So wonder not if our eyes are bright,
And clear as the pearly dew,
So wonder not if our heart's are light
For our wants and cares are few.
Then hey, fal de ral! Who so free?
Oh, the gypsy's roving life for me.
Then hey, fal de ral! Who so free?
Oh, the gypsy's roving life for me.

*At the end of the song,* ISHMAEL *rises, moves behind* NELL *and* ZELLA *to down left centre. He places a hat on the ground and crouches behind it.*

**Ishmael**: Now come, my brothers and sisters. Let us count our morning's gains. Zella – you are the youngest, you come first and show us that which you have earned.

**Zella**: (*rising and moving to right of hat and kneeling beside it*) Here are the bright pieces I made from selling the wooden pegs. See how they shine like stars at midnight. (*puts coins into hat and returns to her place by the fire*).
**Ishmael**: Pharos, my son. (*as* PHAROS *crosses behind* MEG, NELL *and* ZELLA *to right of the hat*). How many hen roosts have you peeped into this morning?
(*General laughter*).
**Pharos**: Three silver pieces in exchange for brown eggs (*puts money into hat*). That is all I made this morning. (*returns to place via upstage of others*).
**Ishmael**: Nell, my daughter whose husband rests in the sky above, what have you for us today?
**Nell**: (*rising and moving to right of hat*) Here's a fine silken scarf. We'll get a silver crown for that 'ere night fall, I'll be bound. (*puts it into the hat*) And here are the coins I earned by selling the wooden spoons I fashioned yesterday (*puts coins into hat and returns to her place by the fire*).
**Ishmael**: Wife?
**Meg**: (*as she rises and moves upstage to right of hat*) Old Meg told many a fortune today. Many a young girl has learned that which she desired to know. I promised them all handsome husbands, tall and straight and no end of children—seven, perhaps eight boys and as many girls. (*chuckles*) Here—(*puts money into hat*) T'was a good morning's work indeed. (*chuckles, returns to her place*).
**Ishmael**: And now for that which I shall contribute. (*takes a pile of coins from his pocket and showers them into the hat—there is a gasp from the others*) I am an old man but I have lost none of my cunning. The old white horse fetched a good price. (*rising and picking up hat—and moving to above fire*) Come now, the midday sun has been opening the flowers long since. We must return to Polstead Fair without delay. Remember that, this very evening, we strike our tents and move on to Sudbury.
**Meg**: (*rising*) Aye, 'tis a good three hours' trek to Sudbury. We must be on our way by six of the clock if we are to reach there before nightfall. Come along!

*The others rise and busy themselves around the camp fire.*

**Ishmael**: In the meantime, we have work to do. Nell, go get the baskets of pegs. Pharos, go see to the horses.
**Pharos**: (*as he exits with* NELL *left*) We go. Come, Nell. I'll give you a hand with the baskets first.
**Nell**: Tis a good fair. There's plenty of rich folk there anxious to part with their silver (*exit left*).
**Meg**: Aye and all wanting their fortunes told it seems. I'll

off to my tent to get my cards and crystal ball (*moves towards exit left*) Tis Tuesday today – a lucky day for gypsy women 'tis said (*exits left*).

**Ishmael**: (*moving to right of* ZELLA) Now, Zella, you know what is to be done, do you not? While we are away at Polstead Fair, you see that all is made ready so that we can depart for Sudbury the instant we return from the fair.

**Zella**: Your bidding shall be done, Father.

**Ishmael**: (*moving to exit left and turning*) By six tonight, all that will remain in this spot will be the cold ashes of our fire and the marks of our vanished tents. Farewell, Zella. We will return 'ere long. (*exit left*).

**Zella**: Farewell! Farewell!

*After they have gone,* ZELLA *crosses to left of the tree stump down right centre.*

**Zella**: (*aside*) Twas most fortunate that 'twas my day to stay behind at the camp and prepare for our departure. Yesterday, when I was in the wood gathering fuel for the fire, I met a fine gentleman. We conversed for a while and he told me his name was William Corder, and that he is the son of the rich squire here in Polstead. When it was time for him to return to his house, he informed me that he would come again today. I cannot wait to see him again for he is most handsome and kind. He said that he desired, most earnestly, for me to tell his fortune and that, afterwards, he would give me something to remember him by. I wonder what it could be. I will sit here and await his arrival (*sits*).

WILLIAM CORDER *enters left and moves to left of the centre tree. He is dressed in the traditional villain's costume* (*top hat, frock coat etc.*) *He carries a riding crop.*

**Corder**: (*aside*) Ah, there is the maiden, resting on yonder tree stump. I watched the other gypsy vagrants go on their way. Now is the girl all alone. She thinks that the purpose of my visit today is to have my fortune told but I have other plans. Indeed I have. Even though she be a gypsy wench, she is most desirable and I mean to possess her. Ha! Ha! Ha! Before this day's sun sets in the sky, she will be mine – mine! (*aloud – moving down to left of* ZELLA) Ah, my dear, I see you kept your promise, eh? You are a good girl, are you not – a good girl. (*aside*) But not too good I trust. Ha! Ha! Ha!

**Zella**: (*rising*) Sir, you have come, as you said you would. I am most pleased to see you again. But you must not stay long for I have things to do before the others return from the fair.

**Corder**: (*aside*) So have I, my pretty one – so have I! Ha! Ha! Ha! (*aloud*) But a few minutes, my dear – but a few minutes.
**Zella**: I think we should proceed to business without delay.
**Corder**: (*aside*) Exactly what I had in mind – exactly. (*aloud*) To tell my fortune – is that what you mean?
**Zella**: Indeed yes, if you still desire it.
**Corder**: (*aside*) Oh, I do, you may be sure. (*aloud*) Most certainly, my dear. Where would you like me to sit?
**Zella**: Here on this tree stump will serve well. I will kneel at your feet so that I may hold your hand.
**Corder**: (*aside*) Better and better! (*aloud*) That is a most excellent idea.

*He sits on the tree stump with* ZELLA *kneeling on his right side.*

**Zella**: Now will I take your hand, but first, mine must be crossed with a piece of silver. Tis an old gypsy custom. Without it the signs would not be clear.
**Corder**: Silver you say? (*fetching a coin from his pocket*) Very well, my dear, you shall have silver (*hands coin to her which she passes across her palm and pockets*).
**Zella**: Now, let me see (*takes* CORDER's *hand and examines it*) Ah – there is something you want. I cannot perceive what it might be.
**Corder**: (*aside*) But you will before long – indeed you will. Ha! Ha! Ha!
**Zella**: Before many moons have waxed and waned, that which you want shall be yours.
**Corder**: (*aside*) I've no intention of waiting that long for it, you may be sure. (*aloud*) What ails you, child? You look puzzled.
**Zella**: I do not understand – it is indeed most puzzling. Your line of life is long. Were I to examine that alone, then would I deduce that you would live to a great age and survive to sit your grandchildren on your knee and kiss and fondle them.
**Corder**: (*aside*) Egad, there shall be another on my knee long before that if I have my way. (*aloud*) What mean you?
**Zella**: When I examine your love line, I see a deep cut across it.
**Corder**: And what does that portend?
**Zella**: That you are to be unlucky in love.
**Corder**: Enough! Enough! I wish to hear no more of your foolish prattle. I believe not in fortune tellers.
**Zella**: But, sir, I thought that was why you had come here today.

**Corder**: I but agreed to please you. There are other matters to be discussed far more important than mere fortune telling.
**Zella**: (*rising*) Very well—so be it if that is what you wish but I assure you that 'tis not foolish. I saw something which disturbs me. I would like to examine you more closely.
**Corder**: (*aside*) And you so shall, my beauty, and so you shall. (*aloud*) Later perhaps, later. But now let us talk about you.
**Zella**: About me? Why should you wish to talk about me? I am but a simple gypsy girl. There is nothing about me that could be of interest to you.
**Corder**: (*aside*) Isn't there, eh? We'll see about that 'ere long. (*aloud*) Tell me, were you born in these parts.
**Zella**: I am one of the wild flowers of the forest. Persecution drives us hither and thither for refuge. We roam the countryside, living in ditches and under hedges with the stars and the moon above for our ceiling. I know not which oak tree, in which forest, bears my certificate of birth.
**Corder**: And how old are you, my child?
**Zella**: I know not. More than two hundred new moons have illuminated the heavens since first I saw their light.
**Corder**: Indeed! Indeed! That is most interesting. Now, my dear, there is something I wish to say to you.
**Zella**: Yes?
**Corder**: Although it is but yesterday since first we met, I vow that you have not been out of my thoughts for one moment since.
**Zella**: What mean you, sir? I fail to understand you.
**Corder**: I am a shy, modest person, not at my ease in the company of ladies, so you must forgive me if I do not express myself as well as I would wish. What I am trying to say is that I have fallen in love with someone.
**Zella**: Fallen in love?
**Corder**: Indeed yes. Can you not guess to whom I allude?
**Zella**: Why, no, sir. Tell me who it is.
**Corder**: Tis none other than the fair maiden who stands beside me now.
**Zella**: You don't mean—you cannot mean—
**Corder**: Yes! Yes! Tis you I love and I desire most sincerely to take you for my wife.
**Zella**: (*turning away*) No! No! Say not that. Tis impossible.
**Corder**: Impossible? Why impossible? Why should that be? Do you not like me—even a little?
**Zella**: (*turning to* CORDER) Oh yes, I like you. Indeed I do.
**Corder**: Then do you not trust me?

**Zella**: With all my heart. The glance of your eyes tells me your heart is good.
**Corder**: Well then? Why should you not become my wife?
**Zella**: You are not one of our race. I have no hope that you can be aught to me, or I to you. For have I not sworn, as all our race have sworn, never to mingle our blood?
**Corder**: (*catching hold of her*) Come away with me. Come away with me now. Forget your stupid vows.
**Zella**: Grasp me not so firmly!
**Corder**: I mean to have you.
**Zella**: Nay—say not so—say not so!
**Corder**: Even though you may not love me now, you will come to do so, I promise you.
**Zella**: Nay! Nay! A gypsy has no love beyond her own race. I will be true to my gypsy vow.
**Corder**: I will make you into a fine lady. I will buy you beautiful clothes.
**Zella**: No! No!
**Corder**: You shall live in a grand house and have servants to carry out your slightest wish.
**Zella**: Never! Never!
**Corder**: Gold, silver—all will be yours, if you but say the word.
**Zella**: No—no—not for the wild, wild world! It cannot be, I tell you! It cannot be!

**Corder**: (*aside*) Curse the girl, she drives a hard bargain! Now must I proceed on a different tack if I am to gain the maiden. (*aloud*) Sit down here for a moment, my dear. I have something of great import to impart.

**Zella**: (*hesitating*) I know not if I should do so.
**Corder**: Come—just for a moment or two.
**Zella**: Very well—just for a moment then. (*sits*).
**Corder**: Now—'tis time I spoke plainly.
**Zella**: Yes?
**Corder**: When last you pitched your tents in Polstead, something most tragic occurred. Did you know that?
**Zella**: No. I cannot recall any such event. I know not what you mean.
**Corder**: Then I will have to tell you, won't I? One of my gamekeepers was killed in this very wood.
**Zella**: Killed?
**Corder**: Killed. I found him by the path that leads to the clearing yonder. The poor man was dying of gunshot wounds he had received. He was beyond aid from any man. He had but a few brief moments of life left when I discovered him.

**Zella**: That is most terrible. Who was the perpetrator of such a dastardly deed?
**Corder**: Do you not know?
**Zella**: Indeed not – why should I know? Twas but a moment since you acquainted me with the happening.
**Corder**: Then must I tell you. It was one of your accursed tribe.
**Zella**: (*rising*) Tis false! Tis false!
**Corder**: No falsehood, I assure you. With his dying breath, he named the villain who had shot him down.
**Zella**: Who? Tell me who?
**Corder**: Your brother, Pharos!
**Zella**: No! No! It cannot be. You lie! My brother is a good man. He would not be guilty of such a deed.
**Corder**: The gamekeeper swore it before he died.
**Zella**: Oh – 'tis horrible – horrible!
**Corder**: (*aside*) The foolish girl believes me. Ha! Ha! Ha! I'll have her yet.
**Zella**: But I fail to understand. If what you say is true –
**Corder**: Alas, 'tis only too true.
**Zella**: Then there is indeed a mystery.
**Corder**: What mystery?
**Zella**: Why have not the officers of the law apprehended my poor brother?
**Corder**: (*aside*) If she believes that which I am now to tell her, she would believe anything. (*aloud*) The explanation is simple enough, my dear. He has not been arrested for the crime because I am a kind, generous man and could not find it in my heart to name him. I have no desire to see him suspended from the gallows tree one fine morning with thousands of wretches flocking to witness his ignominious end. (*he shivers violently and moves to below fire*).
**Zella**: What is it, sir? You look pale.

**Corder**: (*recovering*) Tis nothing – just "someone walking over my grave", as they say. Now – as I was explaining, my kind nature allows me not to hand your brother over to the authorities.
**Zella**: (*going to* CORDER) Sir, sir – what can I say? What can I say? How can I possibly thank you for your silence?

**Corder**: (*aside*) Now am I about to triumph! The girl is in my power and will thus remain until I have had my way with her. Ha! Ha! Ha! (*aloud*) Now, listen intently to what I have to say. I will depart from here 'ere long but return tonight before your tribe decamp. In the meantime, I suggest to you that you weigh very carefully the facts of this matter.
**Zella**: What mean you?

**Corder**: It is very clear. Late tonight I depart for London. If you agree to be the partner of my journey, my lips will be tightly closed for ever. No living soul will ever learn of your brother's crime.
**Zella**: If I refuse to come with you, what then?
**Corder**: Then, before I leave for London, I will pay a visit to the magistrates and acquaint them with the truth.
**Zella**: Oh, no—not that! Not that I implore you!
**Corder**: The remedy is in your own hands. (*moving up left and turning*). I go. Think not to trick me. I am resolved. Farewell then until tonight. (*aside*) The girl is mine! Ha! Ha! Ha! (*exit*).
**Zella**: (*running to exit and calling after him*). Spare me! Spare me! In the name of Heaven, spare me!

*After he has gone she returns to centre stage.*

**Zella**: Oh, woe is me! Woe is me! I am bewildered by my position. My future is too dreadful to contemplate. If I yield not to the villain's demands, then will my poor brother, Pharos, be apprehended, tried and condemned to death. But what is the price of silence? A fate—worse than death! (*moving down left*) When I arose from my bed this morn, I was a happy, contented girl without a care in the world. What am I now? What will be my destiny? I am broken on fortune's wheel. As Heaven is my witness, I believed that man's confession of love. Now what do I discover? I find that he is a vile rogue who would stop at nothing to besmirch me. But my brother shall not die! He shall not swing from the gallows tree. I must make this sacrifice to save one of my tribe. That is the only possible course open to me (*to centre of stage*) Yes—it must be so—alas, it must be so. When the villain returns tonight, I will go to London with him. No matter what the cost, my dear, dear brother shall live! (*noises off*) But what is that? It would seem to be voices I know (*runs to left and looks off*) Tis my father and mother returned, so soon. (*to centre stage*) They must not see my tear-stained face. They must not discover the reason for my dolour. (*moves to down centre*).

*Enter* ISHMAEL *and* MEG *left.*

**Ishmael**: Zella! Why tarry you here? Why have you not started to prepare the camp for our departure as I instructed you to do?
**Zella**: (*wiping her eyes without turning*) I was about to do so. I did not expect your return so soon. (*turning to face them*) Why did you not go to Polstead Fair this afternoon?
**Meg**: A dreadful fire has engulfed all. Not a stick remains —all is lost.

**Ishmael**: (*moving up to centre*) Come now, let us get all together for an early departure. To remain here longer would serve no useful purpose. We will strike our tents and be gone.
**Zella**: (*moving up towards* ISHMAEL) Be gone? But I cannot be gone so soon.
**Meg**: (*moving to left of camp fire*) What mean you, girl? What cause have you to linger here? Answer me!
**Zella**: I cannot say. (*turning away*) I must not go—I must not!
**Ishmael**: (*going to* ZELLA *and catching hold of her*) I say again, what mean you, girl? (*pause*) Speak!
**Zella**: Oh woe is me! Better I had never been born!
**Meg**: (*moving to the right of* ZELLA *via upstage of* ISHMAEL). Tell me, child, tell your old mother the reason for your lamentations.
**Zella**: Alas! Alas!
**Meg**: Tell me—tell me!
**Zella**: I—I . . .
**Meg**: Yes? Yes?
**Zella**: I have promised to marry a gentleman.
**Ishmael**: A gentleman! What gentleman?
**Zella**: A gentleman of this parish.
**Ishmael**: Is he of our blood?
**Zella**: No—no he is not.
**Ishmael**: A gorgio! No! No! That cannot be! That must not be! I forbid it!
**Meg**: (*moving away down right*). You know not what you say, child. You know not what you do.
**Zella**: I have given my word.
**Ishmael**: By the wide Heaven—desist!
**Zella**: (*moving down left of* MEG) Dearest Mother, (*turning to include* ISHMAEL) Dearest Father, you know that I would rather die than cast even the lightest cloud over my tribe. Your merest, slightest wish I have obeyed without question, but what I do now, I do because I must. It is the only way —the only way.

NELL *enters left.*

**Ishmael**: (*moving towards* NELL *left centre*) Nell! Nell! Summon forth your brother! You must both be witness of what I now must do.
**Nell**: (*running off left*) Brother, Brother – come at once! We are bid to attend.
**Ishmael**: (*moving to left of* ZELLA) How could you have the heart to do what you have done?
**Zella**: Heaven knows what is in store for me but it must be—it must be.

**Ishmael**: You will live to rue this day.

NELL *and* PHAROS *enter left and stand left of the fire.* NELL *on* PHAROS *right.*

**Pharos**: What is it, Father? What has happened?
**Ishmael**: Tis Zella, the flower of our tribe, the darling of our hearts.
**Pharos**: What has she done?
**Ishmael**: She has brought disgrace upon us.
**Nell**: Disgrace? What mean you?
**Ishmael**: She has consorted with our accursed enemy, the house people and brought shame upon our peaceful tent. Now is her star an evil one indeed.
**Nell**: Father, Father—blight not the flower you have reared in love and tenderness.
**Ishmael**: Enough! Enough! Speak no more! (*to* ZELLA) By the sun and moon and by my mother's grave, I swear that I disown you.
**Zella**: No! No!
**Ishmael**: I call you not my child.
**Zella**: Oh, say not so! Say not so!
**Ishmael**: You shall never more dwell in the same tents with us.
**Zella**: Pity! Pity!
**Ishmael**: I look upon you as lost to us for ever.
**Zella**: No! No!
**Ishmael**: You will be an outcast from our tribe, false daughter of a lost country!
**Zella**: Kill me—kill me if you will! But do not banish me, I beseech you.
**Ishmael**: No—the sleep of death you shall not have from me.
**Pharos**: Father, Father, have pity on her!
**Ishmael**: (*turning to* PHAROS) Silence! One more word from your lips and I swear you shall be the partner of her banishment.
**Nell**: Father—dearest Father—let your nature turn to her again.
**Ishmael**: Back to your tent, Daughter, before I let loose my rage upon you.

NELL *moves towards the exit left and watches.*

**Ishmael**: Cast her forth! (*there is a clap of thunder*) Cast her forth into the storm! Henceforth we are strangers!
**Zella**: (*running to exit up right*) I go! I go! (*turns to face others*) I know only too well what I have done to warrant your curses. Though I fear we are parted for ever and all my cherished dreams of happiness destroyed, I still have

hope that you will live to be assured how guiltless I am. Remember me sometimes in your prayers. What I do, I do because there is no other path which I may tread. Remember that! And now—farewell Father, farewell Mother, farewell my brother and sister. Farewell—for ever! (*exit*).

*The lights fade and come up again almost at once. There is no one on stage but* WILLIAM CORDER *who is hidden behind the centre tree. The camp fire and tent remain—it is evening.*

*Enter* NELL *from left.*

**Nell**: (*aside*) Twelve months have passed since last we pitched our tents upon this spot. Twelve long months since my darling little sister, the flower of our tribe, brought disgrace upon us and was cast forth. Since that moment, not once has her name passed my father's lips. She is to him as though dead. In his eyes she is no more. (*moving to centre stage*). But this very morning, when I was crossing the pond, by the bridge, hard by the village green here in Polstead, I thought I saw her in the distance wandering as though in a dream. Her clothes were ragged and her hair awry. There was a wild look about her as one demented. I called her by name but she answered me not. I ran to accost her but before I could reach her side, she had gone up the lane that leads to the Red Barn. When I reached the turning, she had vanished as though a ghost. Search as I would, I could not find her. By now, the others of our tribe are locked in the arms of sleep, resting from the toils of the day. I will now to the village to make enquiries about my dear sister. I must proceed with caution for should my father learn of my actions, then should I suffer the same fate and be banished for ever. (*she shivers*) But the night grows cold. I will go first to fetch my shawl, to shield me from the chill winds. (*exits left*).

*After she has gone*, WILLIAM CORDER *steps out from behind the centre tree.*

**Corder**: (*aside*) Curse the girl! I hear that she has found her way back here from London where I left her when I had grown tired of her. I care not if she acquaints her gypsy people with the circumstances for they will remain silent. They are proud and would not share their knowledge with others. But what if she tells my father? All would then be lost for he would turn me out and cut me from his will. I will wait here and see what befalls. (*hides behind tree*).

NELL *enters left and tiptoes across to stage right.*

**Nell**: (*as she moves across stage*). Now to the village and the hoped for news of my sister Zella.

*A figure appears up right in the dim light.*

**Nell**: (*calling in a whisper*). Who is that? Who are you? (*pause*) Answer!

ZELLA *staggers on and collapses on the ground below the tree stump. She is dressed in ragged clothes and her hair is dishevelled.*

**Nell**: (*running to* ZELLA) Zella! Zella! Is that you? (*gently lifts her and leans her against the tree stump and kneels beside her*) Zella! Tis you. But how changed is my darling flower. Speak to me! Speak to me!

**Corder**: (*appearing from behind tree—aside*) Tis true. The wretched girl has returned—she is here! Curses! Curses! Curses! (*returns behind tree*).

**Zella**: (*opening her eyes*) Nell! Nell! My dear sister, Nell! (*closes her eyes again*).

**Nell**: What has happened to you? Tell me what has come to pass. What has brought you to this state?

**Zella**: I am weary to death. I faint with lack of sleep.

**Nell**: (*aside*) What can I do? I dare not take her to my tent. Should my father discover her, he would cast her forth once more. (*aloud*) Come let me put my shawl around you. You are cold and shivering. (*does so*) Now—now—rest in my arms. (*holds her*).

**Zella**: (*gasping*) Dearest Nell—Dearest Nell! How I have suffered, words could not describe (*coughs*).

**Nell**: Now—now—gently, gently.

**Zella**: The villain, whose life I shared in London, cast me out when he grew weary of me. I was alone in a strange city with no one to protect me or look after me.

**Nell**: Cast you out? When—when did he do that?

**Zella**: Many moons ago. I have wandered abroad since then. I slept in ditches, under haystacks and in the woods, living off berries. At last, I found my way back to the village but my strength has left me. I have no will to live upon this earth much longer.

**Nell**: Poor, poor Zella! This man—this vile rogue—why did he cast you out? You were his wife.

**Zella**: No wife—no wife, alas! He kept not his promise to marry me.

**Nell**: Then—then you are . . .

**Zella**: I am a ruined woman. Never again will I be able to hold my head erect. Forever will the blush of shame mantle my cheeks.

**Corder**: (*looking round the tree—aside*) Foolish girl—as if I would have married her—a common gypsy. Forever was she begging me to make an honest woman of her. I tired

of her pleadings and sent her packing. Ha! Ha! Ha! (*returns to behind tree*).
**Nell**: Why kept he not his promise?
**Zella**: Twas a promise made to be broken. I was a victim of his subterfuge.
**Nell**: What mean you?
**Zella**: It is too dreadful.
**Nell**: Tell me! Tell me!
**Zella**: He told me that our brother Pharos, had been guilty of some awful crime.
**Nell**: Pharos! What crime?
**Zella**: The villain told me that Pharos had shot down a gamekeeper. Before he died, this gamekeeper told the villain that Pharos had committed the deed. Then this monster said that unless I went with him to London he would tell his dreadful secret to the magistrates.
**Nell**: Pharos! I cannot believe it. He would not have done such a terrible thing.
**Zella**: Oh no,—he did not—he did not. I know that now but 'tis too late. I was a victim of the villain's awful ruse.
**Nell**: What mean you?
**Zella**: The villain confessed that 'twas but a trick to gain me for himself. Then, laughing as if he was a madman, he threw me out into the night. I—I can recount no more. I am exhausted and o'erwearied. I fear that I may not be much longer for this mortal world. Ere long, my eyes will close forever in the sleep of death.
**Corder**: (*from behind tree—aside*) Then will I be safe—safe!
**Nell**: No—say not so. I will summon forth the others of our tribe. Then will I acquaint them with the true circumstances of this awful business and entreat them to show forgiveness to you. (*places* ZELLA *gently against tree trunk and goes to exit left and calls*) Father, Mother, Brother Pharos, come you here, I beg of you, come this instant. Come! (*returns and takes* ZELLA *in her arms again*).

*Enter* PHAROS, MEG *and* ISHMAEL. ISHMAEL *to right of camp fire*, MEG *on his left and* PHAROS *left of fire*).

**Ishmael**: What is it, Nell? Why call you us from our rest?
**Nell**: Tis Zella. She has returned to us.
**Meg**: Zella!
**Pharos**: Zella!
**Ishmael**: I know not what you mean. I know no person of that name.
**Nell**: Your daughter, Zella. Your younger daughter, Zella.
**Ishmael**: I have no younger daughter. You and your brother, Pharos, are my only offspring.

**Nell**: Father, Father, say not so! Here is your daughter, Zella—this poor, pale shadow is your dear, lost daughter returned to us once more. The villain, who won her from us, has cast her out. Forgive her!
**Ishmael**: Your pleadings are in vain. I know her not.
**Nell**: She is your own flesh, your own blood. Let your nature turn to her again. I entreat you to pardon her and take her back to our tents and to your heart.
**Ishmael**: Waste not your breath.
**Nell**: Mother, dear Mother, if all my pleas are in vain, I beseech you to intervene to restore my sister to her rightful place.
**Meg**: Your father has spoken. His will is mine—it must be. You know that.
**Nell**: (*to* ISHMAEL). She was the victim of a wicked plot. The villain forced her to go with him to seal his lips on some terrible crime he claimed had been committed by one of our tribe.
**Ishmael**: (*moving towards her*) What is that? What say you?
**Meg**: (*following to left of* ISHMAEL) What crime? Speak!
**Nell**: He accused our brother, Pharos, of murder. He said he had the proof!
**Pharos**: (*to down left centre*) Murder! What murder? I have committed no murder.
**Ishmael**: You say that this man claimed that Pharos had killed someone?
**Nell**: Yes—and he used this falsehood to gain our sister's virtue. Now he has turned her out and, laughingly denied the veracity of this claim.
**Meg**: The name—the name of this villain!
**Nell**: I know not. She has not revealed his name to me.
**Ishmael**: (*to left of* NELL *and* ZELLA) Brethren, sisters—our daughter has returned to us and begs for pardon and though we thrust her forth with curses, yet will I take her to my heart again. Daughter, I forgive you.
**Meg**: (*to left of* ISHMAEL) Amen!
**Pharos**: (*to below fire*) Amen!
**Zella**: (*opening her eyes*) Father, dear Father. Words cannot describe the joy I feel to thus receive your forgiveness. It has lightened my heart.
**Ishmael**: You are again my child.

**Zella**: Blessing on thee, Father—blessing. Now can I die in peace.

**Meg**: Speak not of dying. You are returned to your own people. Now must I confess that your name has been oftener on my lips than my prayers. Thank Heaven we can

at last see you clear of this awful sin.
**Zella**: I owe much to you and more than I could ever repay were I to live. But 'tis too late—alas too late. I fear I will not see the grey of the coming morn.
**Ishmael**: This villain—this vile seducer—tell us his name that we may seek revenge.
**Zella**: Tis—'tis—William Corder! (*gasps*) Remember that name—William Corder.
**Ishmael**: We will remember! We will remember!
**Nell**: / **Pharos**: / **Meg**: We will remember—fear not!
**Zella**: My eyes grow dim—I see you but faintly—goodbye dearest Father, goodbye dearest Mother, goodbye my own sweet sister and beloved brother—goodbye. (*she dies*).
**Nell**: She is dead. Our darling Zella is no more.
**Meg**: No! No! (*kneeling on* ZELLA's *left*) Zella! My child! My child!
**Corder**: (*stepping out from behind centre tree*) She is dead and I am safe! No longer can she bear witness of my deeds other than to her wretched tribe. Ha! Ha! Ha! There are other maidens here in Polstead to occupy my thoughts. Only today was I passing along the lane by the cottage of old Thomas Marten, the molecatcher, when I espied his elder daughter Maria—she is a comely wench. Who knows perhaps one day, in the not too distant future, Maria Marten will be my destiny—who knows? Now must I away from this spot before I am observed. (*exits left*).
**Ishmael**: Now, by the stars and moon and Heaven above do I swear vengeance. Vengeance! Come all of you—swear!
**Pharos**: (*producing knife*) I swear before you all that I will not rest until this knife is buried in the villain's heart. As Heaven is my witness he shall die! Death to William Corder!

NELL *places* ZELLA *gently on the grass and points to the camp fire as do the other gypsies.*

**All**: Death to William Corder!! Death to William Corder!! Death to William Corder!!

SLOW CURTAIN

# PRODUCTION NOTES

## STYLE OF PERFORMANCE

The difficulty we encounter when we set about producing a melodrama is that, whereas we understand that the less sophisticated audiences of the 19th century accepted them with a fair measure of credulity, it would be almost impossible to expect a modern audience to take them seriously. How then should a producer tackle them for presentation today?

The first solution might appear to be to burlesque them unmercifully. I do not agree with this method of approach. This style of presentation might work for a short extract but for a full evening's entertainment the joke wears thin very quickly. I have found that the most successful way is to overplay them - that is to say, to use the style of acting we now label 'ham' and to very slightly burlesque those passages where the dialogue is too absurd to be treated in any other manner. But it is very important to remember that the audience must never be aware that you are laughing at the characters being portrayed. It is the high seriousness of the play which causes hilarity. Another thing to look out for is the juxtaposition of overstatement with understatement which should get good laughs.

Movement and gesture should be exaggerated rather like the old silent films. A convention of melodrama rarely used in the modern play is the aside. There are several ways of treating this, but boldness should be the key. The aside given in a stage whisper, with the back of the hand shielding the actor's mouth from the other players, can be amusing and can be used occasionally, but by far the most laughs are achieved by the actor, who breaks away from the characters to whom he is speaking and approaches the footlights and addresses the audience directly while everyone else on stage 'freezes' for the duration of the aside, in whatever position they are in at the time, and the more ridiculous the position the actors are left in during the 'freeze', the funnier it is.

The temptation to play melodrama slowly must be avoided at all cost. There should be a good overall pace so that the audience are not allowed to realise how absurd the situation is before they are whisked on to the next improbability.

To sum up, I would say - paint the scenes boldly with broad strokes. exaggerate, caricature, and do not be afraid of overstatement. To the actor I would say that if you underplay you may be certain that the audience will laugh at you rather than at the character you are portraying, but if you play the part with all the stops out; if you treat this as that unique opportunity to overact almost unreservedly, then not only will you enjoy yourself, but you may be sure that the audience will, too.

## CASTING

In total, the three plays which comprise this work have a cast of 8 men and 8 women but the complete show can be presented with 3 men and 3 women if the cast appear in more than one play. It is suggested that it could be interesting if, for example, the villain in one play was the hero in the next and the heroine the old woman in another and so on. The cast of "The Gypsy Curse" could be increased by using additional non-speaking gypsies if required. The part of Mary in "One Month To Pay" can be played by an older girl — a long blonde wig and make-up can work wonders.

## SETTINGS

This show has been written so that it can be staged in the simplest possible manner. A few cut-outs and very simple furniture would suffice. Alternatively it could be staged more elaborately, if desired, as there are two intervals to effect set changes. The first two plays have similar settings with the third an exterior. If the show was toured round village halls, the entire settings and furniture would go into a small van.

## MUSIC

Apart from the song in "The Gypsy Curse" (the music for which appears in this script) no special music has been written for this show.

The programme, at the beginning of this book, indicates suitable ballads for singing before each play but these, or similar songs, could be interpolated into the action if required.

Mood music is essential in the presentation of melodrama. "Hearts and Flowers", "Chase" music etc. are the sort of thing required. Societies having difficulty in obtaining this type of music should write to the publishers of this play, Combridge Jackson Limited, who will provide the music of "villain" and "heroine" and "gypsy" themes written for the same author's full-length melodramas. These may be performed without additional fee, apart from a small charge for the sheet music.

## FURNITURE AND PROPERTIES

A full list of the furniture and props referred to in the script is given below. Producers may wish to add items of stage dressing but they are best kept to a minimum in this type of play.

### ONE MONTH TO PAY

2 Armchairs (Victorian in style)
A piece of straw (Joe)
Riding Crop (Squire)
Duffle Bag (Tom)
Basket of food (Mary)
Handkerchief (Mary)

## THE DRUNKARD'S WIFE

Kitchen Table
2 Upright Kitchen Chairs
Small Table
Rocking Chair
Oil Lamp (practical)
Sewing (shroud)
Needle and cotton
Walking stick (Mrs. Fernway)
White wig (Sir Eustace)
White beard (Sir Eustace)
Black moustache (Sir Eustace)
Black beard (Sir Eustace)

## THE GYPSY CURSE

Gypsy campfire (crossed sticks and cauldron
with flame effect)
Sticks
Tree stump or log
Large hat (Ishmael)
Silver coins (Zella)
Silver coins (Pharos)
Silk Scarf (Nell)
Coins (Nell)
Coins (Meg)
Coins (Ishmael)
Riding crop (William Corder)
Silver coins (William Corder)
Handkerchief (Zella)
Shawl (Nell)
Knife (Pharos)

## LIGHTING

This is very simple indeed. Details are given at the beginning of each play. There is one light cue in the middle of the final play. Follow-spots for the villain (in red oı green) are very effective. If it is possible to put in old fashioned footlights, these help to re-create the Victorian theatre. Old oil tins, cut in half and painted black make good imitations of the old cowl type 'floats'.

## COSTUME AND MAKE-UP

The Victorian companies were not too accurate to period, often using the same costume for every show, regardless of date. The final two plays could be any period from 1850 onwards, the third is 1820, but the 'villain' costume is traditional - top hat, tail coat, cloak and black trousers. The gypsies should be as colourful as possible. Much can be achieved with head scarves, earings, coloured blouses and long black skirts.

Make-up is fairly straightforward but it should be bold with a tendency towards caricature for the 'villains' and 'the village simpleton'. The gypsies should have swarthy complexions.